A Commemorative Edition Celebrating

Lewis Grizzard

THE LAST BUS TO ALBUQUERQUE

Edited by Gerrie Ferris

LONGSTREET PRESS, INC.
Atlanta, Georgia

Published by LONGSTREET PRESS, INC.,
a subsidiary of Cox Newspapers, Inc.
a subsidiary of Cox Enterprises, Inc.
2140 Newmarket Parkway
Suite 118
Marietta, Georgia 30067

Printed in the United States of America

1st printing, 1994

Library of Congress Catalog Number 94-77579

ISBN: 1-56352-184-9

This book was printed by Quebecor / Martinsburg, WV

Film preparation by Holland Graphics Inc., Mableton, GA

Book and jacket design by Jill Dible

Illustrations by David Boyd

About The Title

In the spring of 1993, Lewis Grizzard underwent surgery on his battered heart for the third time — once again to replace a faulty valve. After nearly fourteen hours of surgery, doctors could not get his heart restarted. Grizzard was more dead than alive, kept breathing only by a slew of high-tech machines.

Several days later, and against considerable odds, Grizzard's timid heart started beating on its own again. His recovery was long and hard, however, and the following year was filled with one medical problem after another. He told a close friend, "I feel like I'm dying a piece at a time."

Finally in March 1994, with infection spreading through his chest, Grizzard ran out of options; his only choices were to either wait for death — maybe weeks, maybe months — or confront it head-on by undergoing yet another heart operation. For a fighter like Lewis, the choice was obvious.

The day before the surgery, doctors explained the upcoming procedure, leveled with Grizzard about his slim odds, and then asked if he had any questions. In classic Grizzard style, with humor and charm, he answered, "Just one: When's the next bus to Albuquerque?"

With love and respect, we have affectionately entitled this commemorative volume THE LAST BUS TO ALBUQUERQUE.

*For Dr. Randolph P. Martin, Lewis's friend and physician,
whose extraordinary efforts gave us all a
little more time with Lewis.*

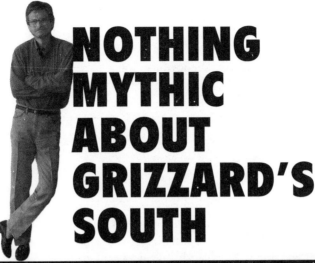

NOTHING MYTHIC ABOUT GRIZZARD'S SOUTH

By Jim Minter

When you have the blues and need something to get your world back on track, drive down Georgia 85 past Senoia to Haralson and Bruce Williams's family grocery.

If you've been there before, they will greet you by name. Bruce, his wife and his mother. They will wrap a package of their homemade pork sausage, famous throughout the land since Judge Griffin Bell served it in Washington, D.C., during the Carter years. He christened it

JIM MINTER

"Rooster Pepper," and told the Yankees it was an aphrodisiac.

It isn't. Bruce's concoction is just good old-fashioned country sausage with plenty of pepper and sage, the kind grandma and grandpa used to make. Despite what some doctors might say, it helps mend certain ailments of the heart.

I had to make a resurrection journey to see Bruce one afternoon last week. I found him wrapping something other than Rooster Pepper sausage.

"You remember our daughter who went to North Georgia College," he said. "She's living in Washington state now, and called home and asked us to save everything that's been written about Lewis Grizzard and send it to her.

"She says you can't believe the interest in Lewis out there. Her friends who know she grew up ten miles from Moreland want to read all the clippings."

That's the way it's been since Lewis's future in the writing business became a question mark. Such a following; proving once again that the American public is often more perceptive than people in high places.

I thought — due to a fortunate set of circumstances — that I knew, understood and appreciated Lewis and his work as much as anyone. I was mistaken. Lewis was a lot bigger than I realized until the gigantic outpouring we witnessed at his death. Not just here. Not only in the South, but across the nation.

Lewis rated a one-column headline at the top of the obituary page in the *New York Times*, which translates into a banner in almost any other newspaper. This is the first paragraph: "Lewis Grizzard, the writer and columnist who recalled the mythic South with folksy humor and nostalgia, died yesterday. He was 47 . . ."

The *Times* went on to do a nice story. But wait a minute! What's this about Lewis's South being the mythic South? I'm not one to bash the *New York Times*. It's a great newspaper. I love to read it. Lewis loved to read it. The editorial page editor of the *Times* is Howell Raines, a fairly good old boy from Alabama, although not exactly a Reagan Republican. Before his migration, Howell was political editor of the *Constitution*, lethal on wayward public servants, bream and bass, and quail on the rise. He favored old dogs, whiskey in a glass, and sometimes dumped peanuts into his Coca-Cola.

I spoke with Howell not long ago and about the first words out of his mouth were: "How is Lewis?" He called him a "helluva talent." I thought that sounded pretty nice coming from the high editor of the *New York Times*, who tilts slightly to the left.

But the "Mythic South" that Lewis wrote about? Lewis's South isn't mythic, at least not yet. Too bad Howell wasn't writing obituaries instead of editorials when Lewis was a subject.

Too bad the critics who misgauged Lewis couldn't have been in Moreland on that Tuesday afternoon.

Somebody — most likely Lewis himself — liked to tell the story about being at a football game when Georgia was playing a team from somewhere else and Lewis was working up a lather.

They told him to relax, that it was only a game. To which Lewis responded: "You don't understand. It's our way of life against theirs!" The *New York Times*, for balance, as taught in Journalism 101, was compelled to mention Lewis's critics, "who found his views on feminists and homosexuals, for example, a throwback to the conventions of the old South."

Well, some conventions of the old South were abundantly evident in Moreland on the Tuesday afternoon when they came to tell their favorite son goodbye.

They came walking to the church, carrying plates of homemade pies and cakes, baskets of fried chicken and bowls of butterbeans. To feed family and friends. The Moreland Methodist congregation doesn't do that just for celebrities. They do it for everyone who makes a last earthly stop on the premises.

They sing the old songs, and hug and cry. They pull off the road and stop their cars when they meet a funeral procession. And in case you haven't noticed, Southern funerals tend to be colorblind.

Moreland folks aren't judgmental. They use good manners, dress up in their best suits and ties and hats, and make the best of whatever it is they are called on to cope with. They don't pick over human frailties.

They take care of their own, and are there when needed.

Moreland doesn't hold a monopoly on these things. The same happens, in one way or the other, in Jewish communities in New York City, in Irish neighborhoods in Boston, and in Polish enclaves in Chicago. This just happens to be the way we do it in the South. We think it's important, and that it works pretty well. We'd like to keep it as long as we can. That's what Lewis was about.

When someone gets around to examining the body of Lewis's work, I think they will find he wrote more about family, friends, school, church and the manners his mother taught him than anything else. That's the South he exalted, and the South he wanted to preserve.

That was the South we saw in Moreland that Tuesday afternoon, and that's why they love Lewis in a little town down at the Meriwether County line, and across the continent in Washington state.

Jim Minter is the former editor of the Atlanta Journal-Constitution.

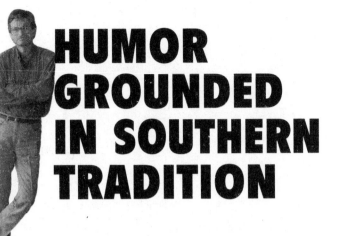

HUMOR GROUNDED IN SOUTHERN TRADITION

By David Goldberg

Many newspaper columnists amass legions of loyal readers and even great wealth during their lifetimes, but few manage to chisel their names into the granite of posterity. Lewis Grizzard may be an exception.

Grizzard won a national following during the presidency of fellow Georgian Jimmy Carter and made his exit with the arrival of another Southern president calling for "change." In the interim he chronicled a South that truly was changing — in reality and image abroad — at blinding speed.

An entry on Lewis Grizzard in the *Encyclopedia of Southern Culture* calls him "among the most successful and insightful contemporary observers of the changing South."

"He is the traditional white, male Southerner confronting the modern world," says Charles Reagan Wilson, who wrote the entry. Wilson is director of the Southern studies curriculum at the University of Mississippi.

"I don't think he could be classified as anything but Southern," says novelist Ferrol Sams, a Fayetteville, Georgia, resident and author. "Even when he wrote about Chicago or Russia it was always from a Southern perspective."

One of Grizzard's favorite Southern traditions was barbecue (pork, of course).

But his writing touched a nerve with readers far beyond the Mason-Dixon Line, Sams and others are quick to point out.

The sophisticates the columnist lampooned may have turned up their noses, but Southern products like Grizzard and country music grew increasingly popular during the 1980s and early '90s.

In a nation grown overly complex and jaded, the South was seen as a cozy corner where it was still OK to express unabashed sentimentality about God, family, country or anything else near to the heart. Grizzard was never too proud to coax tears with an ode to small towns, dogs — regular or Georgia Bull — or Mama.

Roots *In* 1800 *Satirists*

Although some dismissed him as a practitioner of "redneck humor," his style and subject matter sprang from one of the strongest traditions in Southern — and American — letters.

His roots can be traced to the early 1800s, when a number of local humorists in Georgia and Alabama began swapping satirical stories in a variety of periodical publications. These early columnists used "exaggerated characters and peculiar situations," snappy wordplay and hearty samplings of local dialect to lampoon subjects from camp meetings to taverns to well-known families.

The most famous of the early writers was Augustus Baldwin Longstreet, who collected several of these stories in a book called *Georgia Scenes* that is said to have influenced a number of Southern writers. (Several of Grizzard's books were published by Longstreet Press, named for Augustus Baldwin.) "These were entertainments, but they were also social and political satire, usually conservative," said English professor Tom McHaney of Georgia State University, who has made a study of traditional Southern humor. "Lewis's humor is very much in that vein."

The Civil War interrupted that tradition, replacing it with the pathos and sentimentality that dominated in the wake of the South's crushing defeat. Elements of both periods merge in Grizzard's writing, McHaney said.

Another common feature of the old days that lived on in Grizzard was this longstanding principle of Southern story-telling: Never let authorship, or lack thereof, stop you from telling a good story.

A good example is a column reprinted in his book *Kathy Sue Loudermilk, I Love You*, in which Grizzard retells country humorist Jerry Clower's version of a story that Clower says came from then–lieutenant governor Zell Miller of Georgia.

In that tale, Young Harris resident Fuzz Chastain becomes a local hero when he drives his pickup truck loaded with all his family members straight into a burning house. To the amazement of onlookers who had been unable to put out the fire, he and his family leap from the truck and beat the blaze out. In appreciation the townsfolk take up a collection for the Chastain family.

"What will you do with the money?" the mayor asks. Fuzz replies, "I guess the first thing we ought to do is get the brakes fixed on that pickup."

"His early work had a lot of energy and his characters were well-drawn," Wilson said. "Later he became more mean-spirited. He became a caricature of himself as a die-hard, unreconstructed Southerner."

Spokesman For Southern Men

Although Grizzard never wrote a novel with the impact of *Huckleberry Finn*, several observers compared him to Mark Twain: They share newspaper origins, caustic Southern humor and an uncanny knack for self-promotion.

It is the last for which Grizzard may be best remembered: Syndicated in 450 newspapers, he produced twenty books, made several records and — through his non-stop, laugh-filled speaking appearances — became something of a standup comic.

"He's more out of the Twain school [of homespun humor] than, say, Will Rogers," said Lee Walburn, editor of *Atlanta* magazine. Walburn has in his office a pair of bookends with the likeness of Mark Twain on one end and that of Grizzard on the other.

The *Encyclopedia of Southern Culture* regards Grizzard as an important chronicler of a disappearing South.

"He defends the Southern traditions in an age when the small towns of his youth have been enveloped by modern cities such as Atlanta," Wilson writes in the encyclopedia. "He is defined by his sex — a champion of male rights in an age of women's liberation — and his age — a baby boomer who looks back fondly to growing up as part of the Elvis generation."

"Southern men feel somewhat besieged," said Jim Minter, former editor of the *Atlanta Journal-Constitution*, who made Grizzard a columnist in 1978. "The last twenty years they've tried to do the right thing, but they can't seem to please anybody."

But even as he fiercely resisted "modernizing" his attitudes, Grizzard sometimes displayed a disarming tenderness, even fragility, Sams noted.

"People miss the fact that he was really poking fun at himself a lot, which is also a common trait in Southern humor," he said. "That's why his audience identified with him. You can't take yourself too seriously. If you do, you're buying your own con."

David Goldberg is a staff writer for the Atlanta Journal-Constitution.

THAT OL' GRIZZARD MAGIC

By Gerrie Ferris

I remember the night very well. I had gone to an Atlanta restaurant to have dinner with friends. We were halfway through the appetizer course when in walked Lewis Grizzard with a party of six. We were all delighted when his party was seated close enough so we could listen to him hold court, as only he could. His stories were bright, witty and clearly meant for everyone within earshot. It wasn't long before Lewis had nearly everyone around him in stitches and having a great deal of difficulty eating their meals.

W. T. HUNNICUTT JR.
ATLANTA, GEORGIA

Lewis Grizzard was born to storytelling. Yarnspinning Grizzards bequeathed him the voice, the intonation, the timing and the charisma to capture and fascinate audiences. He and audiences had "a thing goin' on." For all the countless times I heard him "in concert," I never stopped being thrilled by the magic of their interplay. And only once in the thirteen years of my association with the entertainer and columnist, did it not

Lewis giving something back to his fans in a live performance.

exist. Only once in my presence did he bomb — although another time a group of preachers got up and left the room after listening to a few slightly naughty preacher jokes. They were not missed.

About the bomb: Lewis was speaking to a group called the Retired Railroad Workers in Savannah, Georgia, in the early 1980s. The banquet room, when we entered, was very quiet for a crowd of around five hundred. Looking over the all-male audience, which we averaged at seventy-three years old, he said, "I have misgivings, Miss Ferris."

It was not pleasant. After the punchline the old guys would titter, but largely, they just nodded. Some looked lost; others went to sleep.

"I can't do it alone," Lewis lamented on the long ride home to Atlanta. "If they're not with me, I'm dead in the water." We later learned half the audience wore hearing aids but their spokesman said they had loved the stories and jokes. And they wanted him back. If he ever went, he never admitted it to me.

I don't know if any of the other Grizzard storytellers turned this oral gift into writing like Lewis did, but as Billy Nelson of Atlanta put it, "If you couldn't get into one of his shows, reading his column was the next best thing."

But not all storytellers are writers. There's a lot lost in the translation from the vocal to the written, and I don't know what forces let Lewis do it, but he did it and without losing any of his unique style. He also kept the same interaction with his readers as he did with his audiences.

People often asked, "Lewis, how come you got so famous?"

Lewis's answer: "My readers made me famous. They think I'm funny and I love 'em. As long as they keep reading and wanting more, I'll give it to them."

Lewis knew what to give his readers. Not all readers, of course, were *his*. The people who made him famous are those who have been dubbed the "silent majority" — a strong constituency and one that has found its voice in a few people, one being Lewis Grizzard.

Once we were in Fayetteville, North Carolina. The concert hall there has two stages. Lewis was to entertain a crowd of three thousand on one stage and a rock group, to be left unnamed, would simultaneously rock 'n' roll on the other. There was, thankfully, a soundproof wall between the two theaters. Before the 8:00 p.m. shows, we sat in a bus eating fried chicken and looking out from the darkened windows over the parking lot as both crowds arrived.

"You can tell which are mine," Lewis said, as the funkily-dressed young separated from the matrons with pocketbooks on their arms and gents garbed in polyester. During the first few moments of the show one of his matrons sitting on the front row slid to the floor in uncontrollable laughter.

I was in a lobby the two theaters shared. The roar coming from Lewis's audience amazed the young crowd wandering around as their band "took five." A girl said to me, "It said Lewis Grizzard (on the marquee) outside. I read his columns sometimes. He's really funny. He does concerts, too? Cool."

His silent majority didn't always agree with him, and they did not remain silent. Lewis occasionally did a column headed "The Mail:"

"Dear Lewis Grizzard:
"My husband and I are big fans of yours. We have bought all your books and certainly have enjoyed them.

But as of this day, neither of us will read your articles or buy your books again. We are tired of the bashing you have given Bill Clinton. Stay out of politics."

Lewis answered back in the column:

"Dear Peggy and Gil:
"Why am I bothering to answer you? You aren't reading me anymore."

There were those readers from the vocal minority who read Grizzard just to disagree and write:

"You should know that outside the compounds of Atlanta the Civil War holds no meaning. The South lost 100-1. Quit crying, quit worrying about the flag, quit building monuments and Tara-lands. It's OVER! PERIOD!"

"Dear Donna:
"100-1? We could have beaten the Yankees with corn-stalks, if they had only been willing to fight that way."

These readers tended to write often."Got another love note from Chris Bolton today," Lewis would say. Chris Bolton was a fanatic Georgia Tech fan. He hated the University of Georgia and Lewis Grizzard, and for years he wrote countless letters saying so. Why, then, did he and many like him write to Lewis all the time?

From his first column to his last, there was an understanding and trust between Lewis and his reader. Readers knew what to expect from Lewis and he never let them down.

They didn't want long, complex words or phrases, soapbox sermons, or boring rhetoric — just short, terse story-telling that they understood. They wanted entertainment; they wanted pathos and sentimentality; they wanted intimacy; they wanted opinions and observations on the day's controversies; they wanted total nonsense; and, yes, like Chris Bolton, they wanted one-sidedness — so they could vent outrage. Lewis rejoiced in it.

"Nobody loves and understands me but the readers," he lamented when his editors suggested that he rethink a controversial column. He knew, though, that what his readers expected and deserved was the truth of his convictions, just as he deserved and expected the truth in their reactions.

All of Lewis's columns were about himself. Eighty percent were also about his mama, his daddy, his ex-wives, his friends, golf, food, Georgia football, traveling, loneliness, zany characters he made up and other oddballs he met every day; and, perhaps readers loved best of all columns on his dog, Catfish, the black Lab. Readers followed Catfish's life from beginning to end, and they felt the pain of loss like he was their own.

Lewis had no children to pass his remarkable talent on to, as Lewis McDonald Grizzard had done to Lewis McDonald Grizzard, Jr., but from what I've heard about Uncle Frank Grizzard, I do hope he has progeny who live to entertain all those within earshot. It would be a shame for the Grizzard magic to go out like the house lights when the show is over.

Gerrie Ferris worked as professional assistant to Lewis Grizzard for thirteen years at the Atlanta Journal-Constitution, *on the road or wherever else The Muse took her. She lives in Atlanta and writes the Q&A column for the newspapers.*

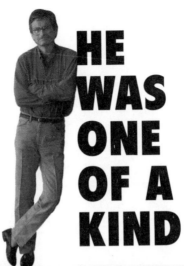

HE WAS ONE OF A KIND

By Robert Steed

My old friend and boon golfing companion, Lewis Grizzard, the Muse of Moreland, Georgia, holed out on Sunday, March 20, 1994. A field marshal in the war on solemnity and against the ever-swelling ranks of the humor-impaired has laid down his baton.

I was pleased to have had a long visit in the hospital with him only a few days before his death, attended his eleventh-hour nuptials, a rousing, lively and therapeutic wake presided over by his physician and friend, Randy Martin, and, finally, the memorial services at the Moreland United Methodist Church. All of these activities, while offering some balm to the premature loss shared by so many, still fell short of closing the chapter on our friendship.

Like all who came in contact with Lewis, I was a victim of "friend abuse" at his hands. When someone made so bold as to publish a collection of my columns under the title *The Sass Menagerie*, Lewis offered a jugular-slicing blurb that read, "With this book Bob Steed has done for literature what Jimmy Swaggart has done for cheap motels." On an earlier, dubious literary enterprise of mine titled *Money, Power and Sex (A*

Self-Help Guide for All Ages), Lewis coughed up the following harumph for the dust jacket — "Bob Steed knows as much about money, power and sex as Boy George knows about testosterone."

However, Lewis could take it as well as give it, and he never seemed to hold it against me when I introduced him at various speaking engagements over the years by saying, "I am always amazed at Lewis Grizzard. I'm primarily amazed because he is one of the few University of Georgia graduates I know who can write sentence after sentence . . . many of them containing both a noun and a verb." It used to confound Georgia Tech graduates when I told them that "Go Dawgs" is a complete sentence.

And, before I get a lot of mail (in crayon) from University of Georgia graduates saying what a towering citadel of scholarship it is, I want to say in advance that I had two daughters who graduated from that institution and both of them, while in attendance, took roller skating for credit.

Lewis also seemed to appreciate the research I engaged in after his first pig valve implant as to what happened to his old heart valve. I learned from some doctors at Emory that Lewis's valve had been placed in the pig's heart and that the pig underwent a severe personality change.

He began wearing little Gucci loafers and glasses, grew a mustache and wound up writing a newspaper column in Atlanta under the name of Ron Hudspeth.

Before the memorial service, one of our mutual friends came up to me and said, "Now that Lewis is gone, you're going to have to write more often." It was a happy thought and I was flattered to hear it expressed, but the chasm left in the 450 newspapers from sea to shining sea that published Lewis's columns is too wide and deep for anyone else to ever fill. Lewis was one of a kind. To borrow a phrase from another humor writer of some renown, the late S. J. Perelman, "They broke the mold before they made Lewis Grizzard."

During the funeral services for Lewis, my mind began wandering back to happier times of golf outings together in Atlanta, Newnan, Augusta (his first outing at Augusta

National), Ireland and Scotland (during our last visit, we talked about mounting a golfing expedition to Spain), and the happy memories began the healing process of pushing aside the somber ones. I even found myself dreaming up typical titles for Grizzard books.

The last one flashed across my mind's eye as the Moreland Methodist choir was winding up on "Precious Memories."

It went, "If Heaven Ain't a Lot Like Ansley Golf Club, Then I Don't Want to Go."

Lewis, we'll miss you. Keep hitting 'em straight.

Robert Steed is an Atlanta lawyer, author, and occasional columnist for the Atlanta Journal-Constitution.

THE FAVOR HE COULDN'T GRANT

By Tony Privett

A few years ago, I asked my friend Lewis Grizzard for a favor. Lewis was, incidentally, an easy mark for people wanting favors. He just didn't know how to say "no."

Lewis made countless free speeches, loaned out thousands of dollars to friends without expecting to collect, and had a soft heart for beggars who looked like they were in genuine need. He also had a well-documented history with women who ran out of his life with large chunks of his money.

But the truth of the matter is Lewis didn't care all that much about money. He enjoyed sharing it.

The real demands on Lewis, like any celebrity, were for his time. Those demands are payback for the fame and fortune.

Nowadays, it's rare to find a personality who will patiently autograph baseballs or books until each and every fan goes home happy. A standing joke in the Georgia bookselling community is that the rare Grizzard books will be the ones *not* signed — a backhanded tribute to the number of days Lewis gave to personalizing all those umpteen thousand books to "Uncle Willie, a great American, and the biggest Dawg fan in Coweta County."

Though not blessed at birth with abundant patience, Lewis was given a double portion of generosity. Those traits would often clash, but in almost every case his appreciation for his loyal readers would prevail and he would sign books for them until his fingers were numb.

I stood alongside many of them who came to say goodbye to Lewis at the funeral home. I watched them come in their red and black, in work boots and fine suits. Though his critics tried to dismiss him as a writer for rednecks, Lewis's readers cut a wide swath across contemporary American culture.

This was abundantly demonstrated by one friend who came to the memorial service in an old car that broke down on I-75. The car was a Rolls Royce. Lewis would've loved it.

Lewis agreed to the favor I asked of him that day, but he was never able to grant it. He promised that if he survived me, he'd write my obituary.

Lewis Grizzard will be remembered for generations for his wonderful sense of humor. But I will keep the memory of the way he chronicled the lives of his friends who passed before him. Friends I did not know but will never forget because of the warmth and grace and celebration of small kindnesses that Lewis immortalized in seven hundred and fifty words. On deadline.

And now I am left to sputter and struggle to try to express the feelings I have about his leaving us so soon. To tell you about the many qualities he had, to try to explain the unseen demons that never stopped stalking him.

He valued loyalty and he returned it. He could find something funny in even the darkest moments and was well-acquainted with the territory.

He was a fierce competitor, as good as Nicklaus on the eighteenth hole with the bets doubled. His beloved black Lab, Catfish, could not have found a better master on this earth.

I am acutely aware that Lewis deserves better than this. If only I'd had a little more time to learn.

Tony Privett was Lewis Grizzard's agent from 1984 until 1990. He lives in Slaton, Texas, his hometown.

"PUT ME NEXT TO MAMA"

By Mike Steed

"There is no cure for birth or death except to try to enjoy the interval."

GEORGE SANTAYANA

When I last produced words for this space, they were about Lewis Grizzard's wedding. I mentioned how surreal the experience was and hinted at the genuine peril he was in. The few short days since have been filled with saying goodbye to this marvelous man who finally ran out of miracles on Sunday, March 20, 1994.

It seems everyone had a personal relationship with Lewis, even folks who had never seen him. He wrote in a style which permitted nearly all of us to feel a part of what he was saying. We could relate. He was either talking for us or, sometimes, talking to us in terms we could understand.

He gave himself one last party. His instructions mandated a wake to be held at his home in Atlanta's Ansley Park neighborhood. And what a wake. I saw few tears. Lewis would have frowned on tears. Friends gathered as they had many times in his home and told tall tales. Dr. Randy Martin evolved into being the emcee and called folks to the front of the kitchen/den to tell a Lewis story. The stories were upbeat, funny — sweet nostalgia.

At the memorial service, the ministers limited their function to prayers and scriptures, although a former pastor of the Moreland United Methodist Church, Rev. Gilbert Steadham, quoted what Lewis told him in a recent visit: "Assure everybody I went to Heaven. There'll be some doubt."

University of Georgia football coach Ray Goff gave a fine eulogy. He began by saying, "What can you say about Lewis Grizzard that you can say in church?" It was almost as if Lewis were goading him to do it when Goff explained how he had come to know Lewis well after winning the "Lewis Grizzard Smart-ass White Boy Invitational Golf Tournament." Yes, he said that in church.

Coach Goff reminded us of how Lewis would take a stand and how he never shied away from writing what he believed, even at the risk of alienating some of his most loyal fans. He allowed as how Lewis might be disappointed so many of us were indoors on a beautiful day wearing a coat and tie and socks.

The eulogy by Jim Minter was, as expected, brilliant. Minter was the hero of Lewis Grizzard. He was the mentor, the surrogate father, the boss, and the inspiration. Lewis both feared and adored Minter. Several years ago Lewis told me, "If the phone rings in the middle of the night, it just terrifies me. My first thought is always: My God, it must be Minter."

As he spoke about his protege, Jim Minter wondered aloud to the congregation, ". . .why it didn't occur to me to get Lewis to write this (eulogy)." He led us in a celebration of the life of Lewis Grizzard and extolled his legendary talents.

Minter acknowledged it was hard to put a happy face on this event. He said, "This world needs Lewis. There's not likely to be another like him." He explained how the loss is so devastating because he believed Lewis's best was yet to come.

We will all miss him — family, friends, fans, and foes. We all enjoyed his interval. He was anything but perfect, but nothing less than real.

Dedra Kyle Grizzard and Lewis were married at Emory University Hospital four days before his death.

In 1991 Lewis wrote a book entitled *Don't Forget to Call Your Mama. . . I Wish I Could Call Mine*. The last words of this book recall a conversation he had with his stepfather, H. B. Atkinson. Lewis wrote:

"I hate to bring up anything like this," he [H.B.] said. "But if anything were to happen to you, what do you want done?"

He was asking me about my funeral.

"There's a place next to your Mama in the cemetery lot," he went on. "Is that where you want to go?"

"Yeah," I answered him with complete assurance. "Put me next to Mama."

And so it is. His ashes are next to Mama. And his memory is in our hearts.

Mike Steed is a syndicated columnist from Bowdon, Georgia.

GRIZZARD WAS SO YOUNG, BUT NOT FOR US TO SAY

By Furman Bisher

Moreland, Georgia — Nowhere is death more emotionally rending than in a small town. In small towns, everybody is everybody else's neighbor. Life is intimate. Any loss is something personal. Grief runs deep. Death in the city is like death on the battlefield. Nothing slows down. Life careens on down its reckless course.

Especially does death gnaw at the heart of a small town when one of its own who traveled far, became a celebrated personality, comes home in a box in the prime of life. What the hometown will never quite realize is that no matter how far the journey, whatever the degree of fame, to return to one's roots is to be absorbed, to be one of the neighbors again.

Moreland put to rest its most famous citizen Tuesday. Lewis McDonald Grizzard, Jr., was too young to be taken out, about half of his life lived. The day before, we had said our farewells to sportswriter Charlie Roberts, who was eighty-three. It has been a saddening week. Charlie had given space in our papers to more young athletes than any person who ever drew a check there. His hat was his familiar trademark, as were Grizzard's sockless feet. (I once sent Lewis a dozen pair of socks from our

Columnists supreme — Lewis and his cohort Furman Bisher.

mill in North Carolina. They're probably still in his drawer.)

I had said to my sister by telephone, "I don't understand. Grizzard was so young. I guess you could say it was Charlie's time to go."

"It is not for any of us on Earth to decide when it is time to go," she said. She is a righteous lady.

Moreland is about the size of my little hometown in North Carolina, and Moreland sat ablaze under a spring sun Tuesday afternoon. All around were signs of a seasonal awakening, blossoming of the red plums, redbuds, forsythia, daffodils or jonquils, or whatever they may have been. Nature was brightening up the sleepy town in honor of its celebrity.

Unfortunately, he didn't make it. He was being cremated in Macon, Georgia, at the time.

This was how Lewis's service differed from those you're accustomed to in a small town. The emotional highlight usually is the opening of the casket for the final viewing of the deceased. Dressed out in their Sunday best in the middle of the week, townspeople file by in solemn ritual, then watch closely as the family gathers around. They want to be able to give a reliable report the next day when anybody asks, "How'd they take it?" as somebody always does.

The hometown choir sang with earnestness the two songs Lewis wanted sung at his funeral, "Amazing Grace" and "Precious Memories." We've all grown up with songs we were taught at the hometown church. Somehow, though, they don't find a place in the mellow part of our being until we've grown older and put distance between us and those compulsory Sunday morning services.

I'll go for "Amazing Grace," but I'd like it played on a bagpipe.

And I've told Josh Powell I want him to take care of himself, for I want him to sing "How Great Thou Art" at my crossing of the bar. My services will require only a small cast.

Everything else would have met Lewis's critical approval, I'd surmise. The ministers leaped to their assigned segment with grace and brevity. Oldtime preachers used to take advantage of a funeral to lay a full sermon on their captive congregation. Ray Goff, Lewis's favorite football coach — not to take anything away from Vince Dooley, who was there — and Jim Minter, Lewis's favorite editor, gave the occasion a proper injection of encomium and humor.

One thing Minter said that struck deep, and makes one feel cheated that Lewis is gone so soon. "He had so many things he wanted to get done," Jim said. "He was already planning his next book."

Well, there isn't much left that hasn't been said about the passing of Lewis. The sun set on Moreland Tuesday, as it usually does. It arose again this morning, as it usually does. That is to say that life goes on. But there is a hollowness in it, not that we shouldn't have come to reason by this time that in the end there is but one winner. Shakespeare wrote it the way it is best said, I guess: "Of all the wonders that I yet have heard, It seems to me most strange that men should fear; Seeing that death, a necessary end, Will come when it will come."

Furman Bisher is sports columnist for the Atlanta Journal.

SMILES, AND THEN SORROW

By Dave Lieber

Ft. Worth, Texas — That summer in Atlanta sixteen years ago, on my very first newspaper job, I discovered the South and hush puppies and Southern belles and okra and pickup trucks and fried catfish.

I also discovered the works of a great Southern writer who explained it all to me: Lewis Grizzard.

The only thing southern in my hometown, New York City, was the South Bronx. The newspapers there didn't carry Grizzard's syndicated column. But reading him for the first time in the *Atlanta Constitution* made me laugh. Out loud. And when you move to a new region, you need to laugh. Get comfortable. Understand your surroundings.

I never met Grizzard (pronounced Gri-ZARD). He worked in the *Constitution's* eighth-floor newsroom; I was a college-intern reporter down on the sixth floor, at the old *Atlanta Journal*. But late one night, after a few beers left me feeling bold, I waited for the security guard to pass on his rounds, then sneaked into Grizzard's office.

Didn't touch anything. Just stood and looked at his big, messy desk. Tried to absorb some of the energy in that room.

Wondered how one writer could make so many people laugh.

Monday's front-page news that Grizzard had died over the weekend of heart failure hit me hard. He was forty-seven.

I knew he was sick. His recent columns told of his hospital stays, his heart operations and his loss of appetite (which he conquered by eating barbecued pork, but only from his boyhood barbecue joint in rural Georgia).

And last Thanksgiving, his dog Catfish, a black Lab, died of a weak heart. Up and died, Grizzard wrote. "My own heart, or whatever's left of it, is breaking," he added ominously.

Monday, I sat at my desk and thought of Grizzard. Of his influence.

Couldn't work. Needed to do something to honor him. But what?

I looked up above my desk and saw "The 1994 Lewis Grizzard Wall Calendar and Guide to Political Incorrectness." I forgot it was hanging there. Filled with sayings and dates important to Grizzard: like Garth Brooks's birthday (February 2), Elvis International Tribute Week (August 7-15). And Sherman occupies Atlanta (September 2).

Just sat there and looked at that calendar. Thought about Grizzard and his dog Catfish. How both up and died.

One thought led to another. Grizzard loved adventures. Loved to travel the rural backwoods.

I'd heard about a catfish place just over the Texas line in Oklahoma, called McGehee's Catfish Restaurant. Located in the Red River Valley, it offers all you can eat and is a favorite of pilots because of its grass landing strip. It sounded like a Lewis Grizzard-type place.

On a whim, I asked the transportation reporter at the *Star-Telegram*, G. Chambers Williams III, if we could ride up there together.

Williams owns a plane. Actually, he owns two. He keeps one near his house, the other near our office. (He takes his job as a transportation writer seriously.)

So that afternoon, the two of us played hooky from work. Climbed into his single-engine Piper Cherokee, the one near the office.

Williams flew us north, past Denton, over farmland and cattle ranches to a muddy bend of the Red River at the Texas border. We landed on the little grass strip beside the restaurant.

Williams is a Grizzard fan, too. Turns out that in 1980, Williams was editor of the Troy, Alabama, newspaper when Grizzard came to town for a college speech. Williams chauffeured him around, and after his speech, Grizzard wanted to go out partying. So they went. Drank long-neck beers, of course.

"That night," Williams told me, "Grizzard said the doctor told him if he quit smoking, quit drinking and quit carousing every night, he'd live a whole lot longer.

"And Grizzard said he asked his doctor, 'Why would I want to?'"

The meal was wonderful. Grizzard would have loved the thin menu ("Catfish Dinner — All You Can Eat — No Doggie Bags, Please") and the worn red carpet and the way the place filled up so quickly with fried catfish devotees, I'm sure he would have enjoyed the juicy entree, the first-rate cole slaw and the crispy hush puppies.

On the flight home, Williams told me how he left Alabama and became editor at six daily and weekly newspapers. At each one, he bought Grizzard's syndicated column and watched circulation increase. "People loved him," he said.

The sun slipped behind the horizon, and I pulled out my Grizzard calendar. "To all you virgins," he wrote for August, "thanks for nothing." I laughed and put the calendar away. It was getting dark. And one of my heroes up and died. And now this silly calendar won't let me forget. Every single day for the rest of the year. It's just too sad.

Dave Lieber is a columnist for the Ft. Worth (Texas) Star-Telegram.

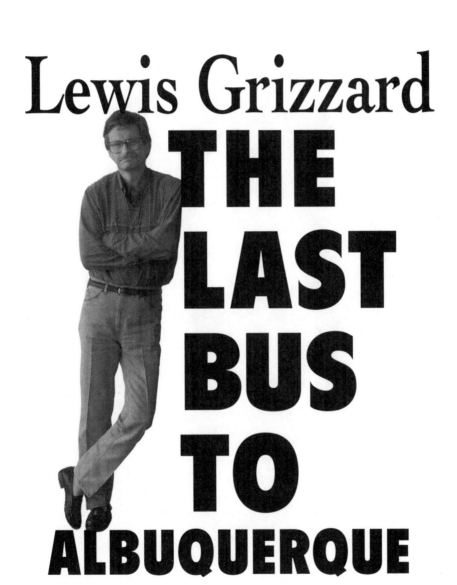

Lewis Grizzard

THE LAST BUS TO ALBUQUERQUE

CHAPTER
One

"Lewis Grizzard was a gift to us. Every once in a while the Lord decides the human race deserves a reward and Lewis was my generation's reward."

PAULA ALLEN
LILBURN, GEORGIA

Marshaling Memories

Darlington, S.C. — I've had some great memories in my life. I played golf with Arnold Palmer, I heard Willie Nelson sing "Precious Memories" in the back yard of the Carter White House. I once took the "Take It Off, Take it All Off" Noxzema shaving cream girl to dinner.

But Sunday.

Sunday I was the grand marshal of the TranSouth 500 automobile race at the historic Darlington Motor Speedway.

I was chosen as the grand marshal because I write a lot about how much I love the South, and there are very few things more Southern than a stock car race.

A politically correct person would have had a heart attack here Sunday. There were more Confederate flags waving in the cool, spring air than were carried across that open field during Pickett's deathly charge at Gettysburg.

Lots of guys drinking beer with their shirts off. Lots of girls you could look at and just know they would pronounce dance as "daintz."

Good people — good people even if they are a little off in the P.C. department.

People with whom I grew up. People I'd still pick if I were involved in anything from a broken beer bottle fight to a rat killing.

So, as grand marshal of the race, I got to tell the drivers on the public address system and on national television they could crank.

Normally, one says, "Gentlemen, start your engines."

I tried a little Southern flair and said, "Gentlemen, y'all can crank 'em up."

It worked. About eight zillion horsepower went off behind me. The ground trembled.

Next, I had to ride in the pace car that led the racers onto the track.

I was in a Pontiac convertible. I was supposed to sit up

on the trunk and wave at the crowd.

A large man got into the back seat with me.

"I'm here to hold you in the car," he said.

Hold me in the car? "We're going to go pretty fast," he explained, "We don't want you getting thrown out of the car."

What have I gotten myself into? So there I am sitting on the back of a car with a man holding my leg and all that horsepower snarling and snorting behind me.

We hit the racetrack. Grit came flying off the track from the car leading us around.

What grit I didn't get in my mouth, I got into my eyes.

I waved at the crowd. The crowd waved back. I'm certain they thought, "Who is this idiot?" We picked up speed. My mouth was full of grit and I was blind. We started at the back of pit row. We pulled off the track and back into the front of the pits. Behind me it sounded like World War II.

The race cars continued on the track. All except one, which had pulled back into the pit with some sort of mechanical problem.

And had its nose on our bumper.

I was three feet from the front of a stock car barreling down on me. "Who was that?" I asked once I was safely out of the convertible.

"They call him 'Swervin' Ernie,' " I was told.

Oh. I watched the start of the race from behind the pit wall, just a few feet from the track. The brightly painted advertising billboards with wheels came by in a near blur. A girl gave me a piece of wax and said, "Bite this in two and put a piece in each of your ears. You can go deaf down here."

Stock car racing, which I hadn't been around since I was a kid sportswriter twenty-five years ago, hadn't changed all that much.

It's still loud, it's still fast, it's still Southern. And it's still the sport of the working man and woman, God bless them all. You be politically correct. I'll hang out with those who say "tars" for tires, take off their shirts, knock down their suds, and love the noise and the furor of stock car racing.

I hadn't realized how much I had missed it.

March 1992

One Boomer Summer

Thirty years ago this summer, four of us went to Daytona Beach, Fla. — the promised land — to look for girls at the pier.

We were all sixteen. We had just finished our junior year in high school. My mother, experiencing a momentary loss of her sanity, let me have her 1958 blue and white Pontiac, which the four of us took turns driving 117 miles per hour toward Daytona.

Like I said, we were there to look for girls and the best place to find girls, we were told, was at the pier where they had a rock 'n' roll band, '60s variety, and the girls allegedly wore very short and very tight shorts.

When you are eight and your parents take you to Daytona Beach, you go to play in the water, build sand castles and play jungle golf.

When you are sixteen you have put away such childish things. It's girls and, lest we forget, beer, too.

The beer, incidentally, was easier to get than the girls.

We got beer the first day in Daytona. It took me three days to find a girl.

The band was playing, "Do You Love Me Now That I Can Dance?" Her name was Kippy. She was wearing very short and very tight shorts.

We danced fast dances.

Then the band, thank God, played a Johnny Mathis slow song and I held Kippy in my arms, and on the walk back to her motel — she was staying with her parents — I kissed her square in the mouth.

Then I went to the beach and I walked on the water.

We had a great time, the four of us. I saw Kippy every night. We never got past kissing, but in those timid times, that was all I had expected anyway.

That was the most fun I ever had.

I was free. I was young. I was experiencing experiences I hardly knew existed.

It couldn't have been thirty years ago, could it? This remembrance was prompted by a jarring thought that came to me recently. Today, I am the same age as the president of the United States. Bill and I are forty-six.

We graduated from high school the same year. We graduated from college the same year. He's an original baby boomer, born in 1946 like me.

Bill Clinton could have gone to Daytona in 1963 and heard the same songs and fell in temporary love with an angel, too.

And, now, he's the most powerful man on earth.

That's frightening for these reasons:

(1) I don't really think I'm mature enough, even at forty-six, and responsible enough to run the United States.

(2) Is Bill Clinton?

(3) If somebody my age is in the White House, it obviously means I'm getting old.

(4) If I'm getting old, it probably means it's time to grow up, and I don't want to.

I didn't have any concrete plans but I always thought I would get some guys and go back to Daytona one of these days.

I guess it's way too late for that now. We would drive the speed limit and the pier is probably gone by now anyway.

I'm a real full-fledged adult, too old for beach trips with the boys. Today's rock 'n' roll is loud and full of rage, and Kippy — we promised to write, but you know about summer love — could be a grandmother.

Deck Sellars, a famous songwriter, wrote this: "Time moves like molasses when you are children, but it rages like a river when you're grown."

January 1993

Singularly Good Southernism Is "Y'all"

A Bill Clinton aide was on television talking about the inauguration of his boss a couple of weeks from now.

He said the theme of the event is, "Y'all come."

I thought "y'all" might be thrust upon the public with the election of Clinton and his running mate, Al Gore.

Clinton, of course, is from Arkansas and Gore is from Tennessee. I don't count either man as having all the characteristics of a true Southerner, since both passed up their state universities for Georgetown and the Ivy League.

But both obviously understand y'all and use it often. I heard Gore unleash many y'alls during the campaign.

Y'all is, to be sure, a Southern thing that most people living outside the South don't understand.

I have long been involved in y'allism. I find it a charming word that is pure Southern, but because it is misunderstood and will be used a great deal during the next four years of the Clinton administration, I thought it would be wise to discuss y'all at some length.

The biggest mistake people from outside the South make in the y'all area is they don't think we say y'all at all.

They think we say "you all."

A Southerner visiting the North surely will be mocked the first time he or she opens his or her mouth and out comes a Southern accent.

Northerners will giggle and ask, "So where are you all from?" I answer by saying, "I all is from Atlanta."

For some unknown reason, Northerners think Southerners use you all in the singular sense. How many movies have I seen where a Northerner is trying to do a Southern accent, failing miserably, saying you all, while addressing one other person.

Southerners rarely use "you all" in any situation but they never, never, ever, ever, use it when addressing just one person.

If you were in my home and I offered you a cup of coffee, I

would say, "Would you like a cup of coffee?" If you and your brother-in-law and your cousin were in my home, then I'd say, "Would y'all like a cup of coffee?" Y'all is, of course, a contraction of you all, and most Southerners use it in all verbal situations involving more than one other person.

And another thing: Northerners also tend to think Southerners say the following when bidding a farewell to a visitor: "You all come back now, you heah?" Maybe the Clampetts said that, but very few real Southerners do.

We might say, "Y'all come back to see us when you can," or, "If y'all can't come, call."

But this "you heah," business is the concoction of some Yankee scriptwriter trying to be cute.

I rarely get into a punching mode, but I was in New York doing a tape version of a book I had written and the producer had hired an actor to speak some of the lines.

"Can you do a Southern accent?" I asked the actor.

"Would you all like to hear me?" he answered.

"I've already heard enough," I said. Then I turned to the producer and said, "This man isn't going to be on my book tape because I will not have the Yankee version of a Southern accent in or on anything that bears my name."

The actor became enraged and said he could, too, do a Southern accent, and I replied, "If you can do a Southern accent, pigs can fly."

We got into each other's face, but before we came to blows, the producer fired the man and ordered him out of the studio and the script was altered so I would be the only one speaking on the tape.

I take the Southern accent and the preservation of its purity quite seriously.

And if any of y'all are going to the inauguration, have a good time. I'd go myself, but I don't want to.

January 1993

A *Barber* To *The* Roots

A male barber cut my hair the other day. I couldn't remember the last time such a thing happened.

I always got my hair cut by a male barber for the first twenty-plus years of my life. Where else would I have gotten my hair cut? The Curl 'n' Chat Beauty Salon? "Hi, Beatrice, see what you can do about these split ends, and did you hear the latest about the Bobbitts? Talk about taking a little off the top."

But at some point during my twenties, somebody — a woman, I'm certain — convinced me I shouldn't go to a barbershop anymore to get my hair cut. I should go to a stylist instead.

So I did. The primary difference between a barber and a stylist, most of whom were women, is that the magazines in the stylists' shops were mostly for women, too, and the stylist charged about three times what the barber used to.

But I kept going to stylists. Somehow, I guess I thought to go back to a barber would be like going back to wearing Old Spice.

The stylist would have an assistant shampoo my hair, first, and then the stylist would, well, style. Barber-cutting, I also noticed, doesn't take as long as styling.

I had a stylist ask me once, "What kind of statement are you trying to make with your hair?" I didn't know how to answer that.

The barber used to forgo the shampoo unless you asked for one, and hair didn't make statements back then. It just sort of sat there on the top of your head in utter silence, especially after the barber had cut it so short about all it could have done was recite the military swearing-in oath.

It's sort of a long story how I got back to a barber for my latest haircut. Let's say only there was a convenience factor involved.

The barber's name was Jack Smith. He has a shop in

Lewis circa 1969, in need of a barber.

Atlanta's Airport Hilton. Jack Smith did a great job on my hair. He cut it the length I like, just touching the ears. He nailed those sideburns that always creep down my cheek when I haven't had a haircut in a while.

When he finished, I looked into a mirror and my hair looked just as good or better than it did after all those expensive stylings I've had.

Vidal Sassoon, his own self, probably couldn't do a lot with my cowlick mop, but that's beside the point.

The point is, it was a nostalgic comfort being back at the hands of a barber. The things I've done in my life to please women, I thought, and I laughed recalling my old barber at home who used to douse on a little Old Spice after my haircut, and say "Now, you smell like a boy dog."

One more thing about Jack Smith, the barber, and my haircut.

Jack Smith didn't turn out to be just Jack Smith. He was the Jack Smith I used to watch pitch for the baseball team that reared me, the old minor league Atlanta Crackers.

THAT Jack Smith. Hard to believe. There I was getting a haircut from a barber who was also a boyhood idol.

In the year 1960, when I was thirteen, Jack was a relief pitcher for Atlanta's Dodger farm team that won the Southern Association's pennant.

We remembered some of his teammates together. Big Jim Koranda. Jim Williams. Pete Richert. Poochie Hartsfield. Tim Harkness.

Jack later made it three seasons in the big leagues.

"But that was when it was a sport, not a business," he laughed, a way of saying he didn't qualify for a pension.

Jack said the fear of flying drove him out of baseball, and he's been cutting hair ever since.

I finally go back to a barber after all these years and he turns out to be THAT Jack Smith.

"I like your haircut," a female friend said to me later.

She probably wouldn't have understood if I had tried to explain it wasn't just a haircut. It had been, as a matter of fact, at least a temporary settling of my restless soul.

January 1994

Karma Broke It

Everything I own breaks, falls apart, gets stopped up or doesn't fit.

It is an incredible phenomenon that lately seems to be occurring even more often than before.

My typewriter broke. It began eating ribbons. Devouring them.

Twisting them. Chewing them and making large holes in them. I was afraid to put my hand down there to try to repair whatever was wrong. I was afraid I might draw back a nub.

I sent the typewriter to a repair shop. The guy there said he thought a small animal might be trapped amongst all the workings.

My air conditioner went out in all this heat. Luckily, I was able to find a repairman who came over in a matter of hours.

He said a cat had got hung up in there and that's why no air would come out.

My car broke down.

"Don't tell me there's a raccoon in my manifold," I said to the mechanic. "That ain't it," he replied. "It's your McPherson strut."

I thought that was a dance.

The doorknob came off my front door. I've got a big brass doorknob on my front door, and one day, I came home, unlocked my door, turned the doorknob and it came off in my hand.

Not only was I standing there with my doorknob in my hand, but not having a pair of pliers on me, I couldn't twist the rod uncovered by the missing knob, and, therefore, couldn't gain entrance into my house.

It is further amazing to me how any time you can't get into your house, you suddenly have to go to the bathroom in the worst way.

I stood on my front porch and did the McPherson strut

until my neighbor came home and I borrowed his pliers.

My shower drain became clogged. It was almost thigh-deep in my shower before I could get a plumber. I thought I was in Des Moines.

The plumber said he thought it was a hairball that had clogged the drain. Everything around me is in a state of utter disrepair and now my hair is falling out. I could eat Drano.

The darndest thing though was the remote control for my television.

It burned.

I'm not going to say there were flames, but I picked it up one day to turn on the television and it was red hot and wouldn't work.

Once it cooled off a bit I took it to the place where I bought my television.

"Never seen nothing like this," said the man after he opened the mechanism and looked at its innards. "Looks like it just caught on fire up in there."

"Is there no possible explanation?" I asked him.

"Act of God, would be my best guess," he answered.

Perhaps all this is spiritual. Maybe it's my karma, or my aura, or my energy or whatever all that stuff people who beg for money in airports talk about.

Maybe I'm hexed or I'm jinxed. I get around it, or it gets around me, and it immediately falls apart.

Or maybe it just seems like that because we live in a world that is a labyrinth of gadgetry. We depend on so much technology, which means there is always going to be something that isn't going to be working.

Nah, that's not it. I'm a jinx. Leave me alone in a room with an anvil and I would figure out a way to render it unworkable.

This goes all the way back to my childhood, by the way. Once, I got a horseshoe game for Christmas and it was a left-handed set.

I'd go lie down, but my mattress is in the shop.

August 1993

My Draft Board Understands

How I avoided the draft:

1961. I had to get a physical before beginning play in a baseball tournament. I was fourteen.

My mother took me to the appointment. My reactions were fine. I had no problems with my eyes, and when I said, "Ahhhh," the doctor didn't find any reason to take out my tonsils.

Then the doctor listened to my heart.

He cleared me to play in the baseball tournament, but he also said I had something he called a heart murmur.

"How serious is that?" my mother asked the doctor.

"Probably nothing to worry about," the doctor answered. "He might even grow out of it."

I didn't grow out of it.

What happened next was I enrolled in the University of Georgia.

1964. I was given a little card saying I was assigned to Air Force Reserve Officer Training Corps (ROTC).

What that meant, I later learned, was I would have to wear a hot uniform to class a couple of days a week, go to ROTC classes and maybe even have to march with a gun on my shoulder.

I didn't want any of that. In the first place I had two jobs. I was a part-timer at the local newspaper, and I was a sports stringer for the late *Atlanta Times*.

In the second place, I didn't like guns. In the third place, I had never flown in an airplane at that point, and I didn't want to fly in one in the future.

My mother had been flown across the country in 1948 in an Army hospital plane carrying her to Walter Reed Hospital in Washington. She was critically ill.

It had frightened her so badly she instilled in me a fear of flying that carries over even until today.

I do fly, but I hate it.

Then I remembered the heart murmur. That was my out.

I went to see the campus doctor and he listened to my heart.

Only he didn't say "heart murmur" like the other doctor had.

He said "aortic insufficiency." He also said I wouldn't have to go into Air Force ROTC.

Vietnam was a billion or so miles away at the time.

1966. I was married. My wife and I went on a cruise of the Bahamas. We met another couple on the ship. He was just out of college and in the Army.

He was going to be sent to Vietnam after the cruise. We received a letter several months later from his wife. He had been killed in action.

Vietnam was on the next block.

But I've got a student deferment and I'm married. I'm safe.

1968. I got an offer to join the sports department of the *Atlanta Journal* when I'm through with school.

Before offering me the job, the man had asked, "What's your draft status?" I told him about my heart and accepted the job. But I wanted to be absolutely certain nobody was going to send me to a jungle to get killed. I went to see another doctor.

He listened to my heart and said, "The military won't take you."

Great news.

"But one day you'll have to get the problem repaired," he added.

Bad news.

"How long before I have to get that problem repaired?" I asked.

"Oh, when you're thirty-five or so," was his reply.

He gave me another note, and I mailed it to my draft board. They gave me a 1-Y status, which meant I was physically unfit for the armed services.

I was six months into my thirty-fifth year, incidentally, when I had my aortic valve replaced.

But I didn't have to step off a helicopter and take a chance of getting shot between the eyes.

I just thought I ought to put this story down as a means of keeping myself out of the Bill Clinton-Dan Quayle draft thing.

September 1992

CHAPTER

Two

"Lewis Grizzard made me laugh, cry, think."

JAMES B. MATHIS, JR.
ATLANTA, GEORGIA

Heartache For The Holidays

New York — Trying to hail a taxi on a street corner in Manhattan at five in the afternoon is like trying to get one buffalo's attention as an entire herd rushes past.

You stand there like an idiot with your hand in the air, and the great yellow procession ignores you and rushes on by.

So I'm twenty minutes into this seemingly futile effort when a blue compact pulls in front of me and stops. There is a sign in the front window that reads: "Car for Hire."

I don't know if this is some sort of renegade cab driver or not, but at this point I don't care.

I climb in the back seat and tell the man in front where I want to go.

He is an elderly man, wearing a hat and thick glasses. We stop at a light as we go through Central Park.

The driver, who hasn't spoken a word to this point, suddenly says, "It was five months today I lost my dear wife."

"I'm sorry to hear that," I reply.

"Five months ago today," he repeats. "It's tough, you know, this time of year."

I imagined that it would be. For all the joy and hope Christmas brings to some, it can mean the searing pain of loneliness to others.

"How long were you married?" I ask.

"For forty-five wonderful years," the driver answers. I'm sure I detect his voice breaking.

The man begins to cry. He takes off his thick glasses and wipes his eyes with his handkerchief. And we're in rush-hour traffic. I'm concerned for my safety, but here's an old man crying over his dead wife a week before Christmas.

He finally stopped crying and put his glasses back on.

"Before she died," he begins again, "she told me I would be OK. She had leukemia, you know. She knew she was dying, but I couldn't accept it. She pulled me close to her and said, 'You're strong as a bull, you can make it without me.' But it isn't easy."

"Any kids?" I ask.

He holds up four fingers. And then he starts crying again. And the glasses come off again and out comes the handkerchief again. This is a terribly delicate situation.

I thought about changing the subject to get my driver's mind off his dead wife and back on the traffic. But what would I talk about — the weather? "I met her in 1944," he goes on. "Ever heard of Roseland?"

"The big dance place?" I ask.

"That's the one. It was big back then. That's where I met her, my wife. I walked in and she was the first girl I saw. She was wearing a white dress.

"I saw her and I noticed she was looking at me too, so I walked over, put my fingers under her chin and said, 'Hello, gorgeous.' That's how the whole thing started. I just can't believe she's gone."

"How old are you?" I ask the man.

"Sixty-six," he answers.

"You're still young," I said, groping to keep up my end of the conversation. "Maybe you will find somebody else."

"That's what she told me before she died. She said I'd meet somebody else. I believe she's up there in heaven looking down at me now. Maybe she's even trying to find someone else for me."

"Could be," I say.

We arrive at my destination. I pay the guy, give him a generous tip and say, "Hang in there."

"I was doing good until Christmas," he says. His voice broke again.

Off came the glasses again. He dried his eyes with the handkerchief again. Then he says goodbye and drives away.

Home alone in New York at Christmas. Only the movies could make it seem like anything but hell.

December 1992

Whiskey Nazis In The Night

It had been a long day. My head hurt. My neck hurt. My stomach hurt. Airplane food.

There had been the long flight after sitting at a typewriter for five hours and also talking to a man who said I needed more life insurance.

I told him what I needed was a beneficiary.

The cabdriver who took me from the airport to my hotel had been sullen. It was raining.

I checked into my hotel. Some silly-looking little man gave me a card I was supposed to put in a slot in my door to get in my room.

Those things never work for me. Whatever happened to metal keys? Before I went to my room, I decided to stop by the bar and get a drink to take up with me.

Just one. It might ease some of the pain and help get me to sleep.

I ordered my drink. The bartender brought it to me. I started to walk out of the bar with it. The bartender said, "You can't take that out of here."

I asked, "Why not?" He said, "It's a rule."

I said, "Whose rule?" He said, "It's just a rule. I don't make 'em, I just follow 'em."

He was just following orders.

Then I knew whose rule it was — the Whiskey Nazis.

I'm against drinking and driving. I'm against anybody not old enough to have studied geometry drinking at all.

But you give the Whiskey Nazis some rope and they'll eventually hang you with it.

"Listen," I went on, "I understand about bars possibly being held responsible when a customer gets smashed and then goes out and runs into something or somebody in his car.

"But I'm just taking this drink up to my room."

"How do I know you aren't going to get in your car with it? There's an open-container law," said the bartender.

"How you know is, I don't have a car here," I explained. "I came from the airport in a cab driven by a jerk. I'm a registered guest here. Here's this little card they gave me to get in my room."

"You still can't take that drink out of the bar," the bartender said.

At that point I realized the simplest thing to do would be to leave the drink in the bar, go to my room, and, if I could get in, order one from room service.

But, like I said, it had been a long day, and I've got a stubborn streak.

"Exactly what are you going to do if I walk out of here with this drink and take it to my room?" I asked.

"Call my manager," the bartender answered.

Probably a guy in jackboots.

I said, "So call your manager."

As the bartender went for the phone, I exited the bar with my drink, took the elevator and went to my room.

My card worked this time, and two minutes after leaving the bar I was alone in the room with my drink and nobody came later and kicked in my door and hauled me off to headquarters for interrogation.

The bartender and his manager didn't know my name or my room number.

I had beaten the Whiskey Nazis.

You can't do this. You can't do that. Where will all this end? I had my drink, went to sleep and dreamed the Speech and Thought Nazis got me for publicly agreeing with Sen. Ernest Hollings.

July 1992

UGA *Glory* Began With Coach Eaves

You look back over your life and you usually see a network of individuals who help you get to wherever it is you happen to be.

There was an English teacher who encouraged my writing. There was another teacher who taught me to type. God knows how hard it would have been to have had to write it all down in longhand.

There was a college dean who taught me to love and honor my profession. And this person got me my first job, and that person saw fit to hire me.

Then there was Joel Eaves. He came close to being the person who changed the direction. He almost made me a PR man.

Coach Eaves. He was tall and silver-haired, with a voice so low and strong, it used to make me think, "That's probably what God sounds like."

Joel Eaves came from Auburn in 1963 to take over as athletic director at the University of Georgia when the department was in near shambles.

There was that mess about an alleged fix of a football game by Georgia's Wallace Butts and Alabama's Bear Bryant. Georgia was averaging three wins a football season and half-empty stadiums in those days.

But enter Joel Eaves, who shocked the state by bringing in a thirty-year-old kid named Vince Dooley to be the new head football coach. Enter Joel Eaves, who could squeeze the green out of a dollar bill and who made the athletic department's financial situation sound once more.

I first met him in 1965. I was a nineteen-year-old kid sportswriter working for the *Daily News* — Athens's new morning newspaper.

I trembled the first time I had to interview him. Walking into his office in the Georgia Coliseum was like walking into an office with the name of Oval.

Lewis coaching his beloved Georgia Bulldogs during the spring game, 1978.

Perhaps Coach Eaves sensed my anxiety. He was patient with me, answering each of my questions, most of which, I am sure, were as sophomoric as I was at the time.

I would interview him often during my last three years at Georgia.

He fed me an occasional scoop, invited my young bride and me on a couple of bowl trips and always treated me with respect, something athletic directors are not known for doing when it comes to sportswriters.

My senior year came along. In early spring Coach Eaves summoned me to his office and offered me the job of assistant sports information director at Georgia. He was willing to pay me $7,200 a year.

I wanted to take it. I wanted to work for Joel Eaves and I wanted to work for Georgia. My bride wanted me to take it. She enjoyed the bowl trips.

But Jim Minter, who was executive sports editor of the *Atlanta Journal* at the time, found me in the Georgia baseball press box a few days later and offered me $160 a week — all the money on Earth — to come to Atlanta and continue as a sportswriter. I took the offer.

Coach Eaves said, "If you ever decide you made the wrong choice, give me a call."

The man died last week. A friend in Athens said, "He just wore out." Coach Eaves had been in a nursing home.

There's been a lot of athletic glory at Georgia the past twenty-five-plus years, and let us all remind ourselves it was Joel Eaves who laid the foundation.

His funeral was at one o'clock Saturday. For a reason. Georgia kicks off at one o'clock Saturdays.

August 1993

Opening A Stretch Of Memory Lane

They opened a new stretch of Georgia 316, a four-lane highway that runs between Lawrenceville and Athens, last week.

What that means is you can drive on four-lane highway all the way between Athens and Atlanta now. From Atlanta, take Interstate 85 to the Lawrenceville exit and then 316 the rest of the way.

"Athens-Atlanta motorists can make the commute in under an hour," a report said.

Twenty-seven blankety-blank years too late, I said.

I was nineteen and a sophomore at the University of Georgia in Athens in 1966. I was also in love, but she lived in Atlanta. We were apart for the first time since the sixth grade.

I had a job in Athens. I worked for the *Daily News*, a fledgling newspaper we struggled to deliver six mornings a week in competition with the afternoon paper that had been in town since movable type was invented.

I worked full time. I went to class, and then I actually worked more than full time. That's because they couldn't run me out of the *Daily News* newsroom, a converted automobile dealership. It remains the best part of my journalism career.

On Saturdays I would go to the newspaper at two, and I would still be there at one the next morning when the Sunday edition was finished.

Then I would get into my blue VW bug and head for Atlanta and my girl. Each week we had from about four Sunday morning until ten Sunday night together. I hated that drive. It was all two-lane from Athens until outside Lawrenceville where I could pick up I-85.

It was forty-five miles of small towns and bends and curves.

Out U.S. 29 through Bogart and Statham. And then into Carl and Auburn, Winder and the infamous speed-trap Dacula.

They never got me in Dacula, but about two o'clock one Sunday morning the night cop got me in little Auburn. He was wearing his pajama top.

But he didn't give me a speeding ticket. The reason he didn't was I gave him the two Georgia-Auburn football tickets in my glove box.

I would fight sleep all the way. A week of classes, studying and work can exhaust even a nineteen-year-old.

Every Saturday night for months, I made that drive. The TLC at the end was worth it, but I still wonder why I didn't doze off one night and run into a tree and kill myself.

We decided to get married the summer of '66. It made a lot of sense. We knew we would marry one day anyway, and I didn't know how many more times I could survive that drive.

So we up and did it. Mama said, "Just make sure you finish school, young man."

My pretty blonde bride got a job at the paper too, and they gave me a raise after we married — from the minimum $1.25 an hour to $1.30. I would have paid them.

When I read about the four-lane being open all the way between Athens and Atlanta, I wondered what if it had been that way back in '66. The drive would have been a lot easier and quicker. Maybe we would have waited to get married. And if we had waited, maybe it would have lasted.

Nineteen is too young to get married. Especially if you're a blindly ambitious, selfish fool. My wife wasn't the one who was the blindly ambitious, selfish fool.

There is a move afoot to give the new 316 connection a name.

"University Parkway" has been suggested.

Somebody else will offer "Bulldog Boulevard," of course, and "Dawg Alley" must be considered, too.

Whatever they name it when I drive it — and I will drive it often — I will think of her and how I blew it and how perhaps a little extra concrete twenty-seven years ago might have kept something that was very good intact. You tend to think that way as you get older.

All that's left to say, I suppose, is drive carefully on Nancy and Lewis's Road.

July 1993

Abstinence The Key To Safe Computing

People look at me like I'm crazy when they say, "I suppose you work on a laptop computer," and I reply, "These fingertips have never, and will never, touch one key on any sort of computer."

"You don't mean to say you write it out longhand, do you?" Is there a next question? I reply to that this way: "Listen, you imbecile, there is only one way anybody should compose and that is upon a manual typewriter."

I then tell them that statement is in the Bible somewhere and they ask me, "Oh, yeah?" And I reply, "Verily."

Then they ask, "Where in the Bible?" And I say, "The book of Royal," and they say there is no book of Royal in the Bible, and by that time I'm halfway down the street and the conversation is over.

I abhor computers. And I don't know how they work, and I don't intend to find out. I believe computers are responsible for a great number of ills in this society.

For one thing, when people screw up today, all they have to do is blame it on the computer. If you screwed up before computers, you had to be clever and imaginative in coming up with a means of covering your tail.

You had to say, "The dog did it," or, "You might not believe this, sir, but I was just sitting here at my desk when a large goat walked in and ate the report you wanted right off my desk."

Ronald Reagan, who was our president, never blamed anything on a computer. When he screwed up, he actually told the truth and said, "I forgot."

Besides all that, since I don't know how computers work and refuse to find out, it could mean computers are magic. That could also mean they are the work of evil spirits, the kind that made Jimmy Swaggart go out and look for hookers.

You get evil spirits involved in anything and pretty soon the economy fails, crime rates go up, politicians begin writing bad

Lewis always preferred the old way, from typewriters to banking.

checks, and all presidential candidates go around blithering like idiots.

And this one other thing. I have steadfastly refused to compose upon a computer because I'm not sure where the words go to when you put them into that electric box and push a button and they disappear from the screen.

"Oh, but you can always call them back up," computer-breaths say to me.

Never say always.

You start fooling around with anything mechanical and something eventually will go wrong with it. A dog could go to the bathroom on a wire in my neighborhood and it could cause a short, and all 417 pages of my new book could be lost forever.

Do you think if Margaret Mitchell had done *Gone With the*

Wind on a computer, and it had all disappeared because of a dog's indiscretion, she would have gone to all the trouble of rewriting *GWTW*? Of course not. She would have killed herself.

When I work on a book, I type it on white sheets of paper with a Royal manual typewriter. I make many copies of each sheet. I keep copies in various rooms of my home. I give other copies to friends. I put others in a vault I rent that is buried five thousand feet underneath Stone Mountain.

I'm not about to lose a book.

And they have said I was crazy and old-fashioned because I wouldn't give way to high-tech.

Well, I told you so. Computer virus.

It's been all over the news that something called Michelangelo, probably an evil spirit, could get into computers and wipe out everything stored in them. Great industries could be brought to their knees.

Kingdoms could crumble. Authors could kill themselves in droves.

I was right. Something can get into a computer and lobotomize it.

The only thing that ever got into my typewriter was a large roach, which I promptly typed to an uppercase death with the dollar and ampersand keys.

As I said, I don't know Bo about computers. But I heard on television that the way a virus gets into one is when an infected floppy disk is inserted into it.

Do they make condoms for computers?

March 1992

Those Hard Times

Mama used to talk about hard times a lot. I didn't pay much attention back then.

I had plenty to eat, a nice warm bed and a dog who came when I called him.

But I can remember. I can remember Mama watching me open my Christmas gifts as a child.

I didn't get the air rifle or the expensive electric train I wanted one Christmas. Daddy was gone and Mama taught in a Georgia public school system in the '50s. That's why I didn't get the air rifle or the expensive electric train I wanted.

I seem to remember what I got instead was a pair of skates and some underwear. I probably showed my disappointment.

Mama noticed and said, "Son, all we used to have when I was growing up were hard-candy Christmases."

Mama grew up on a family budget that was based on what a few acres of red clay could produce. What the family didn't eat, they sold or traded for other needs. A dozen fresh yard eggs for a bucket of syrup.

"All we got for Christmas," Mama said, "was a few pieces of hard candy. Daddy just didn't have the money for anything more."

I can remember her talking with the other adults about the Great Depression, an Excedrin recession.

"Times were hard, but I guess we were lucky," Mama would say. "We didn't have any money, but we had some chickens and a cow, and Daddy was still able to grow a few things. At least we didn't go hungry like a lot of other folks."

Hard times. They come and they go. These are really the hardest times most of the people alive in this country today have ever known. My generation, the baby boomers, haven't known any hard times before. I was able to pay for some of my college, but Mama saved shoe boxes full of ones and fives to help me get started.

Opportunities abounded when I graduated. I went to work

for the *Atlanta Journal* for $150 a week in 1968, when I was twenty-one. My mother made $120 a month teaching first grade in Senoia, Georgia, in 1953.

Since I was fifteen, I've never been out of work, except when I chose to be out of work. I decided to devote all my energy to my tennis game back in 1974, so I quit my job at the *Journal*. No problem. I'd saved a few shekels and my wife worked for the apartment complex in which we lived.

We got free rent. My forehand volley improved dramatically.

When I decided I'd never wind up on center court at Forest Hills, I went back to work. I had no problem finding another job. I got one at the *Chicago Sun-Times* in 1975, making $28,000 a year.

And I'm still one of the lucky ones. I've still got a job today. A lot of other people don't, of course. Unemployment rates are up, to be sure, but we still can't compare these hard times to those of our parents and grandparents.

We're in a hole, but not nearly as deep a one as the country and its citizens have been in before.

What I'm wondering is, are we as strong and determined as our forebears were? They held up and held on and went through hell to get out of the deep well they were in.

Can we stick it out and remove ourselves from a comparative pothole? Perhaps it's easy for me to ask such questions. General Motors hasn't laid me off. My employer hasn't gone out of business.

But all of us have an example that was set by those who gave us life and reared us.

They blamed the politicians just like we're doing. Damn Hoover. Do-nothing Bush.

They hurt. They cried. They despaired.

But they survived. And we can too.

It's in our blood.

February 1992

CHAPTER

"He was like everybody's black-sheep cousin. He stated what everybody was afraid to say."

PHILLIP NORRIS
ACWORTH, GEORGIA

The Stuff Of Legends

Sausalito, California — I just sort of stumbled upon the Mark Reuben Vintage Gallery in this shopping mecca across the bay and past Alcatraz from San Francisco.

One of my credit cards was in some fancy little boutique. I simply couldn't hang around to see what would become of it. So I went outside and strolled past other plastic traps, when I noticed a gallery and a sign out front advertising "Sports Legends and History."

I'm partial to both. I still revere the sports legends of my youth, the ones who didn't have multimillion-dollar contracts, didn't wear ear adornments and didn't have a tendency to pout.

They also never begged off from playing because of a headache. I've written a lot of columns with headaches. It looks like a grown man could still play a ballgame with one.

And history has always fascinated me. Especially World War II. Sometimes I'm sorry I missed it.

So I went inside the gallery. All around me were black and white photographs. The first one that caught my eye was the Dodgers' Sandy Koufax pitching a no-hitter in the '60s. I loved Sandy Koufax.

I kept looking. My God, there was a picture of the 1959 White Sox about to take the field in the World Series.

The first major league baseball game I ever saw was in 1959, the White Sox against the Washington Senators in Clark Griffith Stadium. An old soldier took me to see it.

I could still recognize the players in the photograph with no trouble. Luis Aparicio, Nellie Fox, Ted Klusewski, Minnie Minoso and the rest of the Go-Go Sox.

I couldn't believe what I was seeing. This was my childhood here.

Another of my favorite baseball players was Duke Snider of the Dodgers. I came across a photo of the starting Brooklyn lineup in the 1955 World Series and there was the Duke.

I was nine in 1955, and I was such a fan of Duke Snider I

In 1970, sportswriter Lewis Grizzard attended a Kansas City Royals try-out camp. He was advised to "lose some weight and forget baseball."

named a dog after him. And look at the other Dodgers: Campanella, Robinson, Reese, Newcomb and Hodges — the names came back with ease again.

Thirty-six years later they were still young and strong in the photograph. Some are dead now. That was hard to believe, staring down at their youthful images.

And I thought how these storied boys of summers past had had an impact on my life. I was in my early teens when I decided, if I couldn't be the next Sandy Koufax, I at least wanted to be a sportswriter and be some part of what the sports pages brought me each day.

And history. Churchill, FDR, and Stalin. Robert E. Lee. Ike and Bradley and Patton. Doolittle, Black Jack Pershing. And Teddy Roosevelt and the Roughriders.

"I want it all," I said to the saleslady in the gallery.

"We ship," she said.

Here are the photographs I bought: Koufax and fellow Dodger pitcher Don Drysdale, circa 1962.

The '59 White Sox.

The '55 Dodgers.

A young Arnold Palmer in Augusta.

Patton in the field.

Roosevelt and Churchill.

They will hang in a place of honor in my home to remind me of a time when heroes of a different sort, led, fought and played the game.

Hallowed be their names.

May 1992

Service With A Sneer

I was checking into a hotel one late night recently. The desk clerk didn't give me a key, he gave me a rectangular plastic card.

This wasn't my first rodeo. I had stayed at hotel rooms before, and I knew most hotels now give you a plastic card to open the door to your room, not a key.

There was no bellman on duty at the hour I checked in. It was a small town. The bellman got off at six and went over to eat dinner with Aunt Bea and Opie.

So up the elevator — it wasn't that small a town — I went with my bags to my room.

I read the instructions carefully on the rectangular plastic card.

Insert card into slot in door, it read. When green light appears, remove card and door will open.

I inserted the card into the slot in the door. I am good at following directions. A green light did appear, then disappeared. I took the card out and turned the door handle.

The door wouldn't open.

I figured it out. I had to remove the card while the green light was still on in order to get the door to open.

I inserted the card into the slot again. The green light appeared again. I tried to yank the card out before it disappeared again.

I wasn't fast enough. The door still wouldn't open.

"Fast light," I said to myself. Actually I said something else, but they wouldn't allow that kind of language on the "Andy Griffith Show."

I tried a third time.

No luck.

Wyatt Earp wasn't fast enough to outdraw that stupid green light.

Then I suddenly had to go to the bathroom. Why is it that whenever you can't unlock a door, you immediately have to go to the bathroom? It never fails. You can't find your keys to your house and all of a sudden you feel like you drank a Poland Springs water truck for lunch.

I'm tired. I'm sleepy. I have to go to the bathroom, and I'm standing outside a hotel room with a silly rectangular plastic card that is supposed to open my door, but won't.

I know what I have to do. I have to get back on the elevator, go back down to the lobby, use the lobby restroom and then tell the desk clerk my card won't open my door.

He will, of course, be skeptical. He will look at me like, here is a grown man who can't do anything as simple as insert a card in a slot, wait for the green light, then take out the card and open the door.

And he will be correct.

I found the lobby bathroom, then went to the desk clerk.

"I can't get my card to open my door," I said.

"Did you read the instructions on the card?" He asked me, skeptically. Disdain covered his face. I thought for a moment how good it would feel to remove a portion of that, the portion near his nose.

"I read the instructions," I said. "This card won't open my door."

He gave me a new one. The second card didn't work either, so, finally, the desk clerk had to accompany me to my room. He inserted the first card into the slot and my door opened. It took him three seconds. I had to go to the bathroom again.

"There," he said. "That wasn't so hard, was it?" he sneered. And he did sneer. It was a hotel desk clerk's sneer, the same kind you get from a waiter in a spiffy restaurant when you ask if you can have some ice cream on top of the pie a la mode.

I have brought up this situation before. Hotel people tell me that cards keep thieves from stealing keys and breaking into rooms. Of course they do. The thieves couldn't figure out how to work one of those cards either.

I went to the hotel restaurant for lunch the next day. I ordered pie a la mode.

"Want some ice cream on top of that?" the waiter asked.

The hotel and I are even on sneers.

September 1993

Bills Out Of A Hat

During these difficult economic times many among us are having a tough time making our budgets work.

There are a number of ways to deal with this. A friend of mine has been putting all his monthly bills into a hat. Then he pulls them out one by one and writes payment checks until he runs out of money.

When creditors left in the hat when the money is gone call or write to complain, my friend tells them, "Don't bother me or I won't even put you in the hat next month."

Another acquaintance was unable to pay his credit card bill for a couple of months. When the company called and demanded payment, he said, "Listen, if I had any cash I wouldn't need your card."

Another way to handle your debts is to get a loan from the bank and pay off all your bills. Then, you'll just get one bill a month, the one from the bank.

This method will cost you more money in the end because the bank will insist upon charging you interest. But at least you'll be getting just that one bill each month, which will mean less paper clutter in your home.

It is also easier to stall one creditor than a lot of them.

You can always use the old "the check's in the mail" bit, and say, "Boy, the post office has certainly gone to hell, hasn't it."

You will have to pay the bank back eventually, of course, or it will come and take away something very valuable to you, like your house or car.

But maybe by that time, the hard times will be over and you can get back in the clover and start running up a lot of bills again.

I must say, however, I read recently of an individual who came up with a method of dealing with personal financial problems I'd never heard of before. It had to do with the post office, too.

Robby Doyle Calhoun, thirty-five, lives in an apartment complex in Dallas, Texas.

It seems Robby was sick and tired of all the bills he was getting in the mail.

So, when the mailman, Raymond Bell, thirty-five, showed up at his apartment with his mail the other day, Robby stabbed him in the back with a steak knife.

Said a detective who investigated the incident, he didn't like getting bills. He told the maintenance man the day before, he was going to get the mailman.

As unique as this method is, I don't recommend it. Police arrested Robby Doyle Calhoun and charged him with attempted murder and assaulting a federal worker.

The mailman was treated and released at a local hospital, fortunately, and reportedly said, "And we mailpersons worry about dogs."

Actually, I made that part up, but it does bring up another concern for people who deliver the mail — being attacked for bringing unwanted bills.

What happened in Dallas apparently is just another indication of how the recession is impacting the American public and how frustrated we are that the government has no clue as to how to deal with it.

I'm not suggesting we start stabbing politicians in the back, but isn't that what they've been doing to us, figuratively speaking? Absolutely. So the next time they run for re-election, don't even put their names in the hat.

July 1992

A Man's Home Is His Hassle

I've been trying to get my house decorated the way I want it decorated ever since I moved in three years ago.

I share my house with Catfish, the black Lab, but he has no particular notions on how a house should be decorated.

As long as there are dog biscuits to be carried into the living room and eaten on the carpet, he's happy.

I've been married three times and learned to live with pantyhose hanging in my shower, so I don't mind a few dog biscuit crumbs on the living-room carpet.

When a man moves into a house with a wife, he normally leaves the decorating to her. I did that.

My first wife, operating on a limited budget, did our first house in a Naugahyde theme. My third wife spent more on curtains than my first house cost.

But now, I'm in charge of the decorating and for once I want my house to reflect my own ideas about interior design.

I went through three female interior decorators just like that. I told them all at the outset what I didn't want. "No birds or flowers," I insisted. A man's house should not have birds and flowers all over the place.

Women interior decorators, however, ignore such pleadings of a man.

They think, "What does this creep know about interior decorating?" So, all three of the female decorators came up with fabrics and designs featuring — you guessed it — birds and flowers. One even brought in wallpaper for a guest bedroom that featured large, pink birds who appeared to be flying through The Hanging Gardens of Babylon.

I fired her on the spot.

"No-taste creep" she said, rolling her eyes and pooching out her lips as she twitched her way out my front door.

All I wanted was a house that looked like a man lived there.

Leather. Mega-screen TV. I wanted greens and browns instead of stupid pink birds.

I have a large, framed photograph of Herschel Walker running with a football as he led my alma mater, the University of Georgia, to the 1980 National Championship. I wanted that displayed prominently.

I am happy to report I've solved my problem.

I found a male interior decorator. At first, I was a bit suspect of him.

"You don't live alone with cats and have wallpaper with pink birds ?" I asked him.

The man said he was married with two children and he also had a dog. What a job he has done. There isn't a single bird or flower on anything in my house. He found a large, comfortable green sofa and it sits in front of my new giant-screen TV. The wallpaper in the guest bedroom features a guy swinging a golf club. He spent a mere pittance on curtains, put down new carpet in the living room that is the same color as dog biscuit crumbs, and, for the first time in my life, I have a house decorated as I want it decorated.

And I have an entirely new attitude about male interior designers.

Mine didn't roll his eyes and pooch out his lips or twitch out the front door when I said I wanted the big photograph of Herschel over the fireplace.

What a guy.

April 1991

"C" For Conspiracy

I've always enjoyed a good conspiracy, even if it is merely a theoretical one. I'm not sure who's behind that, but it could have been my mother was frightened by somebody from the Trilateral Commission or the John Birch Society or the Moose Club when she was carrying me.

Give me a juicy news item and I usually can offer conjecture there might have been a conspiracy behind it.

Take the Lindbergh baby kidnapping. Was it simply the work of one person or was it connected to the Monroe Doctrine, the Spanish American War or the assassination of President McKinley somehow? When I was a kid in the '50s, I hated the New York Yankees. The Yankees were always able to make some key trade for a player in September who would then lead them to another pennant.

Guys like Bob Cerv, for instance, which starts with C and that stands for communism. You decide what was really going on there.

There was a recent television show that pondered the question, "Were the assassinations of Robert and John Kennedy connected?" Might Sirhan Sirhan have known Jack Ruby? Were Lee Harvey Oswald and Marilyn Monroe ever lovers? And don't forget the great Yankee Clipper, Joe DiMaggio, was once married to Marilyn Monroe and he now endorses Mr. Coffee coffeemakers and all that starts with C, too.

Ah ha! Now, H. Ross Perot mysteriously drops out of the 1992 presidential race only a few hours before Bill Clinton makes his acceptance speech at the Democratic National Convention.

Perot's announcement also came just a day after the baseball All-Star game in which Ken Griffey, Jr., was the most valuable player.

Ken Griffey, Jr., plays for the Seattle Mariners. The Japanese want to buy the Seattle Mariners. Could a surprise attack on the Kingdome be forthcoming? "Come on, Lewis," you might be saying. "You're stretching things a bit here."

Oh, yeah?

What does Bill Clinton's last name begin with? C, that's what.

On the other hand, when Perot made his announcement, why did President Bush make certain he was out in the wilderness of Wyoming, allegedly fishing? Sources now indicate to me the president did not even bother to bait his hook.

So what was he hiding from? Republicans are famous for dirty tricks.

Did they find out Perot is a secret admirer of Jane Fonda and likes cats, and threatened to blow the whistle on him if he didn't get out? And who amongst us really believes the Democrats are above any sort of monkey business? Did the Democrats find out Perot, as a young man, wanted to become a thespian, and has hung out with known hemophiliacs? Did they learn he also thinks there is an *e* on the end of potato and threatened to ask him to spell chrysanthemum (another word beginning with a C) in a debate among the candidates? And notice also how quiet Ted Kennedy has been about this whole thing, not to mention Anita Hill.

Furthermore, does Dan Rather really know who the guys were who mugged him but is afraid to say? Dan Rather works for CBS, by the way.

And Perot and paranoia begin with *P* and that rhymes with C and that stands for conspiracy.

And do not read the following sentence.

Deep throat. Call home.

And quit staring at me like that.

July 1992

Stop And Smell The Flowers

Why is it the older you get the more you begin to notice things you really never paid much attention to before? Simple things. Quiet things.

Natural things.

It's been that way for me, for instance, with flowers. When I was growing up in Moreland, my Aunt Jessie's yard was the flower capital of the county.

People drove from as far away as Grantville, Corinth and Smith City to gaze at the color show Aunt Jessie's yard put on each spring.

I never paid much attention to her flowers, myself. The only time I ever thought about them was when Aunt Jessie would berate me for tromping through her flowers in search of the baseball I just hit from my yard to hers.

"Get out of those flowers, young man!" she must have screamed at me a million times.

I never understood her concern. There I was practicing to grow up to be Gil Hodges, and how could I continue without my baseball.

Now flowers slay me. The azaleas will be blooming in Atlanta soon.

So will the dogwoods. Their beauty decorates the city in pinks and whites and takes an ol' flower stomper's breath.

This week there have been days that were certainly whispers of spring. It was warm and still and it chased away the dreariness of winter.

I spent one afternoon on the golf course. On one hole, the sprinkler system was wetting the grounds around it.

I smelled a smell I hadn't thought of in years. The smell of water upon dry soil.

I can't describe that smell in words, but I remembered it from when the rain used to hit the dusty dirt road in front of my grandmother's house.

Also, I remembered it from when I would be in my grand-

Lewis savoring springtime in Atlanta, circa 1980.

father's fields, following him as he followed his plow and his mule, and it would "come up a cloud" as the old folks used to say, and the rain pelted down upon the freshly plowed earth and produced that smell again.

I looked up at an absolutely clear, blue sky this week. Its brilliance was remarkable. Up there somewhere was a hole in the ozone layer, but I couldn't see it.

All I saw was a blue so clear and so bright it was like looking into eternity.

It's also difficult to describe the feeling of warmth. It's a secure feeling, somehow. I just sort of stood out there on the golf course and wallowed in it.

When chill turns to warm it may be whoever created all this reminding us an end does finally come to winters of discontent.

This is my forty-fifth spring. But it was only the last several years that I began to take a few moments to relish them.

I vividly remember the first time I really noticed and appreciated the coming of spring. I was on a golf course then, too. Augusta National. I had just turned thirty.

I was covering the Masters golf tournament for the *Chicago Sun-Times*.

I was standing on number 16 on an April Sunday that was spectacular. It was warm and cloudless. There was the green of the turf, the blue of the sky, the pink of the azaleas.

I would be catching a flight in a few hours, back to Chicago. I'd called the office earlier. They said it was snowing.

I stood out there and soaked it all in for the first time. It did something to my soul. It also did something to my future.

I vowed at that moment, I'd never miss another Georgia spring.

Twenty-two days later, I was back home in Atlanta with a job as a typer of words upon blank sheets of paper.

Fifteen years later I am still taking the time to smell and feel the glory of springtime. Getting older does have its benefits.

Sorry about the flowers I stomped, Aunt Jessie. I never learned to hit a curve ball anyway.

March 1992

CHAPTER

"Lewis was one of us. He was from a loving family, and he worked hard from childhood to adulthood to educate himself. He relied on his own talent and perseverance to succeed, always with a positive attitude. Lewis 'dug his own ditch,' made his own mistakes, succeeded and sometimes failed. He was real and unpretentious."

LOVE WILLIAMS
NEWNAN, GEORGIA

Save The 'O'Possum

San Francisco — You walk around in this city and on every corner of every street, it seems, there is somebody with a hand out asking for money to save something.

They're big on saving the rain forests out here.

"Give to save the rain forest," a guy, who looked a little like the spotted owl somebody else is trying to save, asked.

"I gave at the last corner," I said.

"I don't give a hoot," he replied, "You should give at my corner, too. If we don't save the rain forest, there won't be any more oxygen to breathe."

"Well," I said, walking away, "by that time the hole in the ozone layer will have gotten a lot bigger and we'll all be French-fried anyway."

So I saved a little on that corner, but I got hit on the next one from somebody trying to save the whales.

They're trying to save the rain forests, the spotted owl, the whales, the manatees in Florida, and whatever happened to the snail darter? After experiencing this all day, I began to wonder if I were active enough in this area and was there anything I should get behind and try to save.

Just like that, it came to me. I think I ought to get busy and try to save the possum.

What, you might be asking, do I want to save the possum from? From getting run over by some sort of motorized vehicle every time one tries to cross the road, that's what.

I don't have any research statistics to back this up, but I will be willing to bet at least eight out of every ten possums that try to get from one side of the road to the other get smushed by a car, a Greyhound bus, or a pulpwood truck.

I'm not certain how many dead possums I have seen lying smushed in the road in my lifetime's travels around the South, but I'm certain I've seen more possums than dogs or chickens, legendary road-crossers themselves.

When I was a child, in order to keep me quiet in the car, my family would count dead dogs and dead possums on the road. My grandfather would take dead dogs and I would take dead possums and every time we arrived at our destination I had always counted more dead possums than my grandfather had counted dead dogs.

Chickens and dogs, of course, cross the road to get on the other side. Why possums cross the road remains a mystery. Perhaps they are looking for other possums; I'm not Marlin Perkins here.

Whatever, it is up to us to try to save as many possums crossing the road as possible. Some may be saying, "Isn't it supposed to be 'O'- possum? That is correct, and the way possums got that 'O' in front of their names is from crossing the road and seeing headlights and thinking, " 'O' hell, I'm a goner now."

How to save the possum: Put up signs on roads that read: Watch out for crossing possums.

Increase possum awareness so that motorists will be more sensitive and brake when they see one crossing the road.

In places where there is a high concentration of possums trying to cross the road, possum patrol persons would stop traffic in order to allow the possum to cross in safety.

Save the possum. The 'O' stands for " 'O'nly You can Stop the Road Killings."

And watch for me with my hand out at a street corner near you.

May 1992

Happiness Is A Slice Of White Bread

As I look back on my life, the Waffle House seems to have been one of the most consistent things in it.

The Waffle House is always there at the next exit, always open, always ready to throw on a couple of eggs for me and even an occasional T-bone steak.

It is the Waffle House T-bone that is the subject for today.

You can get a T-bone at Waffle House for about five bucks. It's not the thick, juicy cut one might get at Longhorn's in Atlanta, Manny's in Minneapolis, The Palm in New York or the Plaza III in Kansas City, but for the price it's a pretty good little steak.

It comes with a salad, hash browns and two hamburger buns sliced and toasted. I know, white bread.

"If you eat too much white bread, Lewis, it will kill you," health nuts are saying.

I don't care. I was reared on white bread and I'm going to stay with it. Just get somebody to sing "Precious Memories" at my funeral.

I pulled into a Waffle House the other day off an exit on I-20 between Atlanta and Augusta. It was lunchtime and there are always too many screaming small children in McDonald's.

My Waffle House waitress was named Kay, and she was pleasant — another consistent thing about Waffle House. They have good help.

I ordered the T-bone medium well.

"What kind of dressing do you want on your salad?" Kay asked me.

I knew her name was Kay because she was wearing it on her blouse.

"Ranch," I answered.

"What are you drinking?" Kay went on.

"Iced tea."

Kay wrote all that down and then yelled to the cook: "T-bone, medium well."

The cook, I noticed, never responded, but Waffle House cooks never do. Waffle House cooks have wonderful memories. They can be frying six eggs, four pieces of bacon and have two waffles in the iron at the same time and listen to three waitresses yelling out orders and it all registers and they rarely get an order wrong.

There ought to be a lot of ex-Waffle House cooks in Congress. Maybe they wouldn't forget what the voters elected them to do.

I ate my salad. Then my steak and white bread and hash browns came. My steak was cooked perfectly. I ate all the steak I could cut off the bone with a knife and fork. But did you ever notice how much meat is left on a T-bone steak that you can't get at with a knife and fork? Right next to the bone there's some really great-tasting, tender meat. If you are eating at a fancy steak restaurant, you wouldn't dare think of picking up what's left of your steak and gnawing that good meat off the bone. But this is a Waffle House. The jukebox is playing a fine country tune and how I would like to get to the rest of that meat.

I called Kay over.

"What," I asked, "is the Waffle House policy on a customer picking up what's left of his or her T-bone and gnawing the meat that's close to the bone?"

"Do whatever floats your boat," smiled Kay.

I picked up my T-bone and happily gnawed away.

The guy with the Harley Davidson T-shirt seated at the counter next to me never looked up; nobody in the entire Waffle House seemed offended. What a nice experience. It was just like home. Which is the only other place I've ever picked up a steak and gnawed away at the bone.

A precious memory at the Waffle House. How it will linger. Pass the white bread and somebody put another quarter in the jukebox.

August 1992

Some Things Cannot Be Prepared For

I occasionally still think about the late Charlie Bohannon, Scoutmaster of my Boy Scout troop in my hometown of Moreland.

We met in the little block building across the railroad tracks a quarter-mile from my house.

Charlie always had the stub of a cigar stuck in the side of his mouth. He also had time to deal with all us rowdies. We went camping on the Flint River one time and John Cureton climbed a tree and wouldn't come down.

Cigar in mouth, Charlie finally had to climb the tree and bring John down. The problem wasn't that John was in the tree. He was in the tree singing at the top of his voice and nobody could go to sleep.

Scouting was a great experience for me. Ol' Charlie had some old-fashioned values and he passed them along to some of the rest of us. Boy Scouts don't steal, for instance.

I once passed up a golden opportunity to steal some watermelons from somebody's patch. I felt I'd be letting Charlie down.

Charlie was a good husband, father, provider and Scoutmaster. He touched a lot of little country boys' lives.

I started thinking about Charlie Bohannon and Scouting when I began reading about the efforts in San Francisco to get the Boy Scouts of America to lift its ban against homosexual Scouts and leaders.

The BSA also bans girls and atheists. My entire Moreland troop would have enjoyed being in the Girl Scouts because of the possibility of sharing a tent with Kathy Sue Loudermilk, but I can't imagine a girl wanting to be in the Boy Scouts. You've tied one knot, you've tied them all.

I received my God and Country Award in the Boy Scouts. Let an atheist be a Boy Scout and he would want just a Country Award and the Boy Scouts don't offer that.

As far as homosexuals being Scouts or Scout leaders is

concerned, you must realize you're dealing here with a forty-five-year-old man who simply can't imagine such a thing.

I can't imagine having had a homosexual Scout leader or homosexual fellow Scouts. The reason is, I'm like Charlie Bohannon. I'm terribly old-fashioned, or I'm "politically incorrect," as old-fashioned is called today.

I do admit some members of my troop had doubts about Arnold Bates, the teacher's pet, until somebody saw him kissing Kathy Sue Loudermilk square on the mouth during a Baptist hayride.

But I don't want to overreact here. I doubt there would be that many instances of one Scout trying to have a homosexual relationship with another if the Boy Scouts allowed gays.

And just because a homosexual is a Scoutmaster, it doesn't mean he's also a child molester.

Still, Scouting holds to basic values and standards, and that is its right. Homosexuality is not a basic value or standard. It's an alternative way to live and love.

To each his own.

Now get this. The United Way of the Bay Area, which donates hundreds of thousands of dollars a year to local Scouting units, has threatened to withhold its funds if the Boy Scouts won't change its rule about homosexuals.

Why would anybody want to financially blackmail an organization that does so much for young people? That's a lousy example.

And also get this: Buford Hill, Western region director for the Boy Scouts of America, has said the United Way threat will not change the Scouts' policy against homosexuals.

He said the Western region will look for other sources of financing. And then he said, "Our values are not for sale."

Ol' Charlie Bohannon would have been proud of that statement.

February 1992

Southern Pride Battered And Fried

My hero and professional role model, *Chicago Tribune* columnist Mike Royko, had an astounding piece recently.

(And if this is stealing a column idea, then at least I'm stealing from the best.) According to Royko, at an auto plant in Normal, Illinois, an executive asked the company that ran the plant's cafeteria to offer some more variety.

"Man cannot live by tuna patty melts alone," wrote Royko.

So the cafeteria people decided to offer some Southern cooking one day. They picked the wrong day.

The Friday before the Monday that was the holiday honoring Dr. Martin Luther King, Jr.'s birthday, the cafeteria was to serve barbecue ribs, black-eyed peas, grits and collards.

Two black employees at the plant, Royko further explained, went to see the executive and complained such a meal, just two days before Dr. King's birthday, was a stereotyping of black dining habits. They threatened a boycott of the meal.

The executive, who was also black, ordered the Southern dishes be stricken from the Friday menu. Meatloaf and egg rolls were served instead.

What is astounding to me is, in our search to become politically correct and more sensitive, in this one instance at least, food became an issue.

Southern food. Which has come to be known as soul food.

And my food, too.

I think it is very important to point out barbecue ribs, black-eyed peas, grits and collards may, in fact, be a choicy dish to many black Americans. But it also sounds pretty darn good to me, a white man.

I grew up on soul food. We just called it country cooking. My grandmother cooked it. My mother cooked it.

Friends cooked it. Still do. I might not have made it through my second heart operation if it hadn't been for the country cooking of one of the world's kindest ladies, Jackie Walburn, who delivered to me in the hospital.

And my friend Carol Dunn in Orlando has served me many an enchanting spread featuring her wonderful roast pork.

My Aunt Una cooked me fried chicken, speckled-heart butterbeans, turnip greens, mashed potatoes and creamed corn as recently as Thanksgiving eve.

The creamed corn, the best I ever ate, was provided by my Aunt Jessie.

I scour the world for this kind of food. You can get it in Atlanta at the Luckie Street Grill. And try Atlanta's Colonnade for great beef tips and rice.

Hap Towns will serve you the best pan-fried cornbread you ever tasted in Nashville, and I've driven miles out of the way to taste the country cooking at the New Perry Hotel in Perry, Georgia, hometown of Sen. Sam Nunn.

Don't tell me serving food like that is an affront to the memory of Dr. King. What it would have been in Normal is a celebration of the sort of cooking that has been prevalent in the South, both for blacks and whites, for two hundred years.

Royko asked, "Next Columbus Day would it be an insult to serve spaghetti and meatballs?" What a plate of hogwash, and I can get by with that. I have a pig valve in my own heart, and I can eat my share of barbecue ribs with anybody, black or white or whatever. The best on Earth, by the way, are prepared by Dan Tolbert in Americus.

To charge stereotyping over food trivializes the King holiday. The man didn't give his life for something like that.

It's silly and it's stupid and it makes me want to throw up. Had I eaten meatloaf and egg rolls for lunch, I might.

January 1992

Turkey Man

Every Thanksgiving season I think about him, the man who lived on the property adjacent to my family's in little Moreland when I was a child.

I won't name him. With all those lawyers advertising on television these days, one needs to avoid any bait whatsoever for possible legal action.

But he raised turkeys. Lots of them. A lot of turkeys probably don't smell any worse than a lot of chickens or goats or even dogs, for that matter, but try telling that to the olfactories when the wind suddenly turns east and replaces the scent of Aunt Jessie's petunias with that of heaps of gobbler goo.

We never had turkey for Thanksgiving at my house. Each year my mother would say, "I think I'll bake a hen for Thanksgiving. Turkey is just too dry."

I'm not certain if she really thought turkey was too dry, or if it was the lingering smell, or if it was because my grandfather, her father, never got along with the turkey man.

They were constantly in some sort of dispute. My grandfather was a kind person, not easily riled. He didn't like Jehovah's Witnesses coming to his door and he didn't like opera singers on "The Ed Sullivan Show" (he favored dogs jumping through hoops and the guy with the spinning plates), but he endured Ike spending what he thought was too much time playing golf at Augusta and the soaring price of mules with a minimum amount of grumbling.

The turkey man could set him to boiling, however. The turkey man was burning some trash and the fire spread across my grandfather's side of the fence. World War Moreland nearly broke out.

My grandfather heard some bullets zinging over his head as he plowed his fields a few days later. He was convinced the turkey man was shooting at him.

They would never make friends, and never would have, but my grandfather, who died in those same fields when I was thirteen, did live long enough to see the turkey man lose an even larger conflict, however.

The Moreland Baptist church, across the dirt road from my grandfather's house and just a few hundred yards from the turkey man's, decided to install chimes.

The chimes would play your favorite hymns on Wednesday afternoons before prayer meetings, and then again on Sunday mornings and evenings.

We Methodists thought, "The Baptists are showing off again," but we enjoyed "Rock of Ages" ringing through the air as much as anybody else, if the truth be known.

But not the turkey man.

The chimes hadn't been in for a week when he complained to the church they made his turkeys nervous, and they were losing weight.

I did notice that upon another wind shift, the smell did suddenly seem a bit worse than before due, perhaps, to what turkeys might do even more often when they are nervous, but it was a private opinion I never shared with the adults.

The conflict raged on and on.

The turkey man said he was losing revenue, the church said the chimes had nothing to do with it, and my grandfather smiled knowingly each time he heard "Revive Us Again," and computed lost turkey poundage.

I left home before there was any settlement and I doubt there ever was a settlement.

The turkey man either died or moved on. And age and rust and disinterest eventually stilled the chimes, and I guess all the turkeys shriveled away to nothing.

I suppose all this is why I don't need a big fat turkey on the table at my house to consider it a successful Thanksgiving.

I even had spaghetti once for Thanksgiving.

"I hope this is OK," said the cook. "I didn't have time to do a turkey."

"It's fine," I replied, "Even bad spaghetti doesn't smell."

November 1993

CHAPTER

"He reminded us of the days when it was OK to get choked up listening to the Star Spangled Banner, when the flag was something to be revered...when women were the only people who had body parts pierced...and he reminded us that a game day in Athens is as close to heaven as some folks will ever get."

Rick Williamson
Stone Mountain, Georgia

Seeing Weyman Would Be A Dream Come True

Monroe, Louisiana — Daniel Brantley is fifteen. He's been blind since birth. I met him a year ago in his hometown of Shrevesport.

I made a public appearance there. After the show, Daniel's mother brought him backstage.

I do not mean for any of this to be self-serving. It was just something about Daniel Brantley. He asked me questions about my work and my life I couldn't answer.

He wanted to know where I was when I put this book or that book on tape. He wanted to know who the announcer was on the tape.

He asked me about names and places from columns I'd written years before and had completely forgotten about.

Then he wanted to know about my boyhood friend and idol, Weyman C. Wannamaker, Jr., a great American. "Mr. Lewis," he began, always the polite one, "is Weyman C. Wannamaker, Jr., here with you?"

I said, "I'm afraid not, Daniel."

"I really wanted to talk to him," he said.

"I'll say," added his mother. "For his birthday last year he invited his friends to come dressed like they thought Weyman might look."

I would have enjoyed seeing that. Weyman would have, too.

Where did Daniel get this interest in me and what appeared to be an interest in humor in general? We cut a comedy album in Shreveport that night. We decided to dedicate it to him — "To Daniel Brantley, my No. 1 fan."

I saw Daniel again here in Monroe. Because of Daniel and his remarkable zest for life and laughter despite his blindness, I did a thing here for the Louisiana Center for the Blind. I met another remarkable person, Joanne Wilson, who is the director of the center.

She's also the mother of five and has been blind herself since she was sixteen.

"What we do at the center," she was telling me, "is try to change the image of blind people. The image we want to lose is that of the blind beggar on the street.

"The center teaches blind people self-esteem, work skills and independence. We prepare them to live better lives, to be worthwhile employees," said Joanne Wilson.

"What we want to do is set them free."

Set them free.

The deal I did here was to raise money for the center's summer program for blind children. The center wasn't going to be opened for the children this summer because it couldn't afford it.

But a lot of kind people in Monroe came through for us. The reason I said "us," is that they have named the summer program after me. I've never been so honored.

After the show, Daniel came backstage again and did his impressions of Presidents Nixon, Carter, Reagan and Bush for me — and damned fine impressions they were.

Prediction: This young man will be on a stage himself one of these days.

I saw Daniel again, and I met Roland and Andrea and Chico and many others, all blind children who want what the rest of us want — a fighting chance.

Before Daniel left he asked me, "Are there any good eye doctors over there at Emory Hospital in Atlanta where you had your heart surgery?" Amazing.

"I don't know," I said to him. "Why do you ask?"

"Well," he said, "maybe one day I can have an operation like you did on my eyes and be able to see."

I'll mention to Weyman to include Daniel's dream in his prayers, too.

April 1992

Look Away, Look Away . . . And Mind What You Say

I certainly agree with all those who protested the playing of "Dixie" at a football game in the new Georgia Dome.

Although slavery isn't mentioned in the song, it still makes people think of the Old South, where every white person owned African-American slaves.

"Dixie" is definitely a politically incorrect piece of music. Even the word is offensive to some, and I apologize to those who are offended by my use of it.

But I'm proud to say my alma mater, the University of Georgia, whose current football team has come down with a major case of fumbleitis, years ago rid itself of any connection with the song or the word you-know-what (see, I didn't use the word that time, as I despise offending people).

The Georgia band used to play the song at football games. But not anymore. The only place they still play the song is at the University of Mississippi.

They also wave Confederate flags and they allow prayer before a football game.

I'm not certain how long it will be before members of the Speech Police move in and shut down such reprehensible behavior, but it could be any day now, or at least a couple of days after President Clinton's inauguration.

Georgia not only stopped playing the song, it even changed the name of the band, formerly known as the Dixie Redcoat Band. It became simply the Redcoat Band.

That prompted my stepbrother, Ludlow Porch, the famous radio talk-show personality, to fire off a letter to the editor suggesting the following: "I applaud the dropping of 'Dixie' from the name of the University of Georgia band, but let us not stop there.

"How can we allow the word 'red,' which stands for communism? And the word 'redcoat' itself is an affront to the memory of all those Americans who fought against the redcoats of England in the Revolutionary War.

"And 'band.' Poncho Villa had a 'band' of desperadoes and we had to send brave young soldiers into Mexico after him. So 'band' should go, too, and that just leaves 'The,' which is a dumb name for a large number of musicians, so I guess they're just out of a name altogether."

I believe if we really try we can wipe away all symbols of the Old South forever.

There's a company in Savannah that makes Dixie Crystal Sugar. Sorry, it's just Crystal Sugar from now on, and don't give me any grief about it.

And there's even a Dixie Highway in the South. It should be referred to from now on only as Highway. As in, "Well, you take Highway, then go down three blocks and. . . . " There are even some people named Dixie, believe it or not. They will have to get new first names, or go by their middle names. And if anybody named Dixie lives on Dixie Highway, the Speech Police will likely demand they be shot.

And if the song and word "Dixie" are symbolic of the Old South, I guess we ought to stop using "Old South" as well.

Instead of saying "Old South" perhaps we can refer to it as "Back Then," and we can roll our eyes when we use it so everybody will know we aren't talking about when dinosaurs roamed the Earth, but when slaveholders used to go around singing songs like "Dixie" and "Eating Goober Peas."

But wait. "Eating Goober Peas" is a song from Back Then, too, so don't anybody dare play that at a football game.

Rap songs about killing innocent people, incidentally, are just fine.

September 1992

The Boys Of Summer Go Under The Dome

Baseball season came to a rather rotten end for me in 1991. There I was in Minneapolis's house of horrors, the Metrodome, covering the seventh game of the World Series between Atlanta's Braves (with apologies to the *Portland Oregonian*) and the Minnesota Twins, a nickname a clever person said was insensitive to couples who couldn't have children.

Around the fifth inning, with no score in the game, the ribbon on my typewriter, which was manufactured sometime around the turn of the century, suddenly wouldn't advance. I couldn't make letters and words appear on the white paper in front of me.

I fiddled with the problem for six more outs and was nearing a panic stage. What if I couldn't figure out a way to free the ribbon? The game would end and I would have to write my column longhand and I hadn't written anything in longhand since my last essay-type test in college.

And whom could I get to help me with the ribbon? Everybody else in the press box was writing on a Star Wars computer. Who would remember about typewriter ribbons? By the grace of God, I finally hit the right lever inside my typewriter and the ribbon started moving again.

Then the Braves lost 1-0 because Lonnie Smith went brain dead on the base path.

I finished my column and left the Metrodome. Outside, Twins fans were celebrating by doing such things as climbing onto the tops of buses. I had hired a car and driver to take me back to my hotel.

Some kids had asked my driver for whom he was waiting.

"Some guy from Atlanta," he told them.

When I arrived at the car the kids began heckling me.

"We beat your [bad word]!" one screamed.

"Go home, you redneck!" screamed another.

Once I was inside the car and had locked my doors, they banged on the windows and roof and one of the Norse waifs pressed his nose and mouth on one of the windows.

As I recall the incident now, I think he looked a little like Paul Tsongas.

When I finally reached my hotel, shaken but unscathed, the bar was closed.

I made a mental note that Minnesota calling itself the gopher state was an insult to gophers, and went to sleep.

It is difficult for me to believe the 1992 baseball season is upon us so quickly.

Wasn't the nightmare in Minneapolis just yesterday? Indeed not. The 1992 Atlanta Braves, defending National League champions, are about to open their season, and many questions arise.

I will attempt to answer some of them: Can the Braves repeat as National League champions? Sure.

You really think so? If you really must know, I'm extremely concerned about Cincinnati.

What can we expect of David Justice this season? A lot of pouting when things don't go his way.

Does the team have a drug problem? Well, they were drug all over the field during spring training but you can't really go by that.

Will the chop come back? Was Custer surprised at little Big Horn? Will Jane and Ted have a successful marriage? Who do I look like, Dear Abby? Let's stick to baseball.

What part of the Braves do you think will be the most improved? Their bank accounts.

What would you like to see out of Lonnie Smith this season? An apology.

If the Braves get to the World Series and have to play the Twins again, would you go back to Minneapolis? If I can take along a typewriter technician, and my own bat.

April 1992

The Dipstick And The Great American

The trend away from full-service service stations has affected me a great deal.

I'm not certain exactly when just about every service station started making you pump your own gas. I guess it was back in the early '70s during the oil crunch.

I'm a bit of a dipstick when it comes to doing anything more with a car than turning on the ignition and pressing the gas pedal.

It's not that I'm above pumping my own gasoline, but it sort of makes me nervous. I'm never quite certain how to work the gas nozzle.

My greatest fear is that the gas nozzle won't automatically shut off like it's supposed to when the tank is full and gasoline will spill out all over the ground and all over me and some guy will toss a cigarette away and I'm instant-fried Buddhist monk.

There's something else, too. There isn't anybody around to wash your windshield anymore, either.

If they're going to make you pump your own gas, certainly nobody is going to be friendly enough to come out and ask, "Want me to get that windshield?" And, even on the rare occasions you find a full-service service station, if the attendant does attempt to clean your windshield, he will do a lousy job. He will spray a little cleaner on your windshield and then run over it once with a squeegee and leave a lot of film. Instead of getting the bug goo off, he simply will smear it. Nothing worse than smeared bug goo.

All that is to say I stopped into the Gulf station on Peachtree at the entrance to Ansley Park the other day and I met Melvin Slaughter, an attendant there. He had a shirt that had his first name sewn above his left breast pocket.

Melvin told me he was twenty-eight and he was from Macon and he had been working at the station for three years.

Melvin Slaughter, as it turns out, is a great American.

I was in my red Blazer. I told Melvin to fill it with unleaded. He did, and then without my asking, he washed my front windshield.

A friend had borrowed the Blazer recently to drive to St. Louis. Half the bug population between Georgia and Missouri was dead on my windshield.

Melvin didn't wash my windshield. He attacked it. He sprayed on the cleaner and ran the squeegee through twice, and then he wiped the film off with a paper cloth. But there was still some serious bug remaining, so Melvin got another paper towel, and one by one, he got the bugs off.

I mean he dug down there deep. Elbow grease, they used to call it.

Melvin simply refused to leave a single spot on my windshield.

Then, if that wasn't enough, he went to the back window and did the same sort of job. I said to Melvin, "That's the best job I've had done on a windshield since gasoline was thirty cents a gallon."

Who was president then, Harry Truman?

Melvin replied, "I just try to do the best job I can do. That's what they pay me for."

Melvin Slaughter made my day. Made me think perhaps friendly service isn't dead and gone. Made me feel like a person can still take pride in his or her job, no matter if it is doing his or her best to get bug goo off a windshield.

Isn't that what made this country great in the first place? Absolutely. That and unlocked restrooms.

I sort of miss them, too.

September 1990

A Burger By Any Other Name

I ordered a cheeseburger at lunch the other day. I had never eaten at this particular restaurant before, and whenever I am unsure about the quality of the food at a place, I always order a cheeseburger.

How many ways can you foul up something as simple as a cheeseburger? The bread can be too hard, or the meat might not be cooked to your liking, but that can be fixed quite easily.

After I ordered my cheeseburger — medium well with a soft bun — the waiter asked me, "Do you want a plain cheeseburger or one of our specialties?" There is such a thing as a specialty cheeseburger? A cheeseburger is a piece of hamburger meat with some cheese on top of it served on a hamburger bun.

A pork chop is a pork chop and a cheeseburger is a cheeseburger.

I asked the waiter to elaborate.

"We have a Cajun cheeseburger," he began, "with spices and cooked onions. We have a chili cheeseburger, and you can also have gazpacho on that.

"We have a Swiss cheeseburger, a Monterey Jack cheeseburger, a diet cheeseburger — with just meat and cottage cheese on the side. And we have a mushroom cheeseburger."

I was astounded.

I said to the waiter, "I'm not certain in which book it appears, but I know that somewhere in the Bible it says, 'Thou shalt not put mushrooms on no cheeseburger.'" It's just not the right thing to do.

If I had wanted Cajun food, I would have ordered red beans and rice. If I had wanted chili I would have ordered chili. And gazpacho looks like pond scum.

I hate Swiss cheese, Monterey Jack sounds like a California beach bum, and at 166 pounds, I'm certainly not on a diet — and I wouldn't eat cottage cheese even if I were.

Why do we do this sort of thing? Why do we take something as pure and simple as the cheeseburger and go fiddle with it? I think we should have kept telephones black. I still see no need for designer undershorts.

Who decided to take the numbers off watches? Who decided to make modern shower knobs so complicated? Why does baseball have a designated hitter? Why do we say brunch instead of late breakfast or early lunch? Why did Cadillac change the Seville and ruin it?

What was wrong with Jane Pauley in the morning? Didn't corn flakes, Wheaties, Rice Krispies and Cheerios give us enough of a choice of cereals? Who changed "light" to "lite?" Why are electric typewriters the size of Plymouths? Why do potato chips come in a can?

And why must we have pats of butter in those individual little packages that are so hard to get open? Who said it was OK for lawyers to do television commercials? I told the waiter I wanted a plain, as-God-intended cheeseburger and a Coke.

"Classic, I assume," said the waiter.

"In a six-ounce bottle," I answered.

September 1990

CHAPTER

Six

"He cherished his mama as a queen and his dog as a champ... ."

AMY E. ROBINSON
ST. SIMONS ISLAND, GEORGIA

Lewis's mother, Miss Christine.

Shuttle Off To Civilization

New York — I had a ticket on the Delta shuttle between LaGuardia and Washington's National Airport. Flights leave every half hour.

I'm not certain exactly how long it would have taken me to make the entire trip, hotel-to-hotel, but figure I would want to leave my New York hotel an hour and a half before flight time.

Then figure with time on the runway before taking off and then the time in the air, it likely would have been another hour to Washington.

Then add another forty-five minutes — and I may be underestimating here — for the time between leaving the plane and getting to my Washington hotel.

We're talking three hours and change.

But somebody in New York, knowing of my love affair with trains, suggested I take the Amtrak Metroliner instead of the air shuttle.

It leaves New York's Penn Station on the hour, southbound to Union Station in Washington.

I decided to take the train. I have always maintained trains are the most civilized of all modes of travel.

It took only fifteen minutes to get from my hotel to Penn Station. A redcap was standing at the door. He took my bags, put them on his cart, actually smiled, and said, "Follow me."

We went down into the station, down an escalator and he took me directly to my Metroclub seat. The train left exactly on time at 11 a.m.

The car attendant handed me a card that gave me four choices for lunch, which is included in the $146 one-way ticket.

"You're going all the way to Washington," he said, "so just let me know when you want to eat."

The car wasn't crowded. I had a comfortable seat, a single, next to a large window. There was at least twice the leg room of a plane.

Lewis boarding the engine of the fabled Southern Crescent, 1979.

We stopped at Newark and then at 30th Street Station in Philadelphia. The scenery between New York and Philadelphia is mostly urban decay. But at least you could see something.

A well-dressed man took the seat across from me in Philadelphia. The car attendant welcomed him aboard and asked about his preference for lunch and then said, "Now, if there's anything you need just let me know."

Later, the conductor came by. The man who got on in Philadelphia remarked to him, "The attendant is certainly a pleasant person."

"Yeah," said the conductor in a heavy New York accent, "I think he's from the South."

I had my lunch in Wilmington. It was beef tips, green beans and pasta.

"If you don't like this," laughed the attendant, "you have my permission to go slap the cook."

I liked it. The meat was tender, the green beans had actually been cooked more than three minutes and the pasta was tasty. It beat airline food.

We stopped in Baltimore and then pulled into Washington at 1:55 p.m., exactly as advertised.

Union Station was remodeled a few years ago. It is clean, it is convenient getting to and from trains. It's a visitors' center and a museum. Our government has done something right.

I was off the train and through the station and into a waiting car in less than ten minutes. I was checking into my Georgetown hotel ten minutes later.

From hotel-to-hotel, New-York-to-Washington, it had taken me less than four hours. The trip was pleasant and free of hassle, not to mention, thank goodness, crazed gunmen.

Speaking of our government, I figure it has the same business running a railroad as a whale does in a jewelry store.

But in that Washington-New York corridor it offers a means of travel that isn't that much slower than by air, as well as a good meal and much more comfortable seating.

There was a banner, I noticed, hanging in Union Station in Washington. It read something like, "Amtrak's Metroliner — the civilized shuttle."

Indeed.

December 1993

Old Booger Nose

I got old the other day. I ordered a Glenn Miller tape off television. That's a sure sign the aging process has settled in for good. First of all, if you're not old, why are you still up at the hour they advertise musical tapes from the '40s while you're watching a black and white movie with Stewart Granger or a young Richard Widmark? It's either because you're not sleeping like you used to, or you can't run with the big dogs anymore out there in the neon arena.

And instead of listening to current musical offerings, you've gone and ordered a tape from your parents' generation because it's nostalgic, because you can understand the words when somebody sings, because Glenn Miller music never suggested killing anybody or anything and because it reminds you of a time you actually knew what was going on in the world.

I wasn't born when Glenn Miller died, but I listened to his music as a child on the radio and I saw my late parents jitterbug to "In the Mood" once.

And I've seen *The Glenn Miller Story* about a thousand times on that same late-night television.

Jimmy Stewart was magnificent as Glenn Miller, and aren't all we lost males of divorce, now in the summer of our years, still looking for June Allyson in the Madonna era? So my Glenn Miller tape came in from Time-Life music.

The TV offer wasn't good in Nebraska, or was it New Jersey? I'm not certain why there's usually one state left out when they advertise things you can order on late-night television, but thankfully, they never seem to leave out Georgia.

I had to make a two-hour drive alone, and I decided that would be a perfect time to enjoy my tape for the first time.

There wouldn't be anybody younger than me in the car to ask "What on earth is that?" and to demand that I remove the tape and listen to a rock station, a practice that always makes me nervous and irritable.

I pulled onto the interstate. It was raining. Large trucks

roared past me, leaving walls of water upon my windshield, something else that always makes me nervous and irritable.

Then my tape began.

The first selection was the immortal "In the Mood." It made me want to jitterbug like my mother and father, and I relaxed and forgot about the trucks.

Next was "Pennsylvania 6-5000." That was June Allyson's New York telephone number in *The Glenn Miller Story* and Glenn was so smitten by her he wrote a musical piece about her telephone number.

Love was like that in the '40s.

Today, there's too many digits in a phone number to write a love song about one. "Pennsylvania 1-800-485-6234."

The hits kept coming.

"Moonlight Becomes You." What a lovely thought.

"Sunrise Serenade." Soft and sweet.

"Don't Sit Under the Apple Tree." Lovers asking each other to be true until the war is over.

"Chattanooga Choo-Choo." I enjoyed the piece, but I cringed at the political incorrectness of "Pardon me, boy."

All the greats were there, including "Little Brown Jug," which set me to bouncing around in my seat.

A kid with an earring and his hat on backward passed me. He probably thought I was in rhythm with rapper "Booger Nose" and his recent hit, "I'm Gonna Kill Your Dog."

So, I'm old.

There are benefits, including being able to listen to nonviolent music, being satisfied with a living room couch instead of a bar stool, and realizing I can make it on four or five hours sleep instead of the eight or nine of my youth.

And the young women will be calling me "mister." But I still believe I'll run into June Allyson one of these days, and she'll invite me to go sit under an apple tree.

Yo, June. I'm in the mood.

September 1992

Seersucker Meets Gucci

As my close friends can verify, I am quite fashion-conscious. A regular clothes horse. I seek to be dressed correctly for all occasions.

My formal evening attire, for instance, is always impeccable. For one thing, Harvey, the guy over at the tux rental place, always sees to it any cummerbund I get has no soup stains on it from a previous wearing. For a more casual look I prefer the seersucker jacket I bought in 1964 for fraternity rush, the khaki slacks I wore on the bus to Panama City, Florida, on my first honeymoon, and my faded blue Izod shirt — the one my third wife gave me for Christmas, the same year I gave her a new stepladder so she wouldn't have to borrow one from the neighbors when she cleaned the gutters.

Because I am such a slave to fashion I always look forward to Easter because I can don my white Gucci loafers again.

As anyone with taste knows, one should never, ever wear white until Easter. I've had my white Guccis for several years now. How I scrimped and saved to buy them.

Every extra dime went into my white Gucci account. When I finally had enough money I went to the Gucci store, accompanied by an armed Wells Fargo guard, to purchase them.

Desmondi, the Gucci footwear consultant, went back to the store safe and brought out the dazzling loafers.

You should have heard the "ooooohs" and "aaaahs" when I placed them on my feet and went for a test walk.

"Bravo!" gushed Desmondi.

"Prego!" I said. "Prego" is Italian for "eat my dust." These weren't shoes I was wearing. These were a Ferrari tearing down the Appian Way.

I'd wanted white Guccis since I had seen a pair in the Gucci store in Florence during a European vacation.

I wasn't able to purchase them at the time, however, due to the fact my wife had already worn the writing off my credit card in previous stops in Paris and London.

I was also short of lira because the guy at the glass factory in Venice insisted on cash for the glass gondola my wife insisted I buy her or she wouldn't clean the gutters anymore.

But I vowed one day to own a pair of white Guccis and to wear them without socks, a trend I started at the University of Georgia in 1966 when I discovered black, over-the-calf men's hose had gone to $3 a pair.

White Guccis with no socks do make a rather bold fashion statement: casual, but elegant.

So I went through my clothes the other day and took out my white Guccis and made preparation to wear them to Easter brunch.

I removed a wad of fossilized gum from the sole of the left shoe. I apparently picked up the gum when I last wore my Guccis Labor Day eve at my club's End of Summer Dance, featuring Eddie Corn and the Cobs, who did a mixture of old favorites such as "Satin Doll," as well as modern tunes such as "The Theme From ABC News."

It came back to me. My companion for the evening — a young lady I had met in the hardware store who was shopping for a new stepladder for her gutter-cleaning business — had popped in a piece of Juicy Fruit just before the last dance to the band's romantic rendition of "Jeremiah Was a Bullfrog."

Yes, the moment soon will be at hand when I can put on my white Guccis once more and become the envy of all the fashion-conscious.

Forget the Italian Stallion. The Gucci Kid rides again.

April 1992

Leave Pulitzer Out Of This

I have called this press conference to announce I am not going to retire.

"Why not?"

I need a job.

"But there must be other reasons?"

I don't have $46 million in the bank and I need the company health insurance, are two that come to mind.

"But you have to sit around trying to think of column ideas all the time. That must really become a grind."

Sometimes. But I don't have to do any heavy lifting.

"But what about all the pressure?"

What pressure? If I mess up, nobody dies.

"But what if you write a lousy column? All those readers see it."

They can always read "Dear Abby."

"Aren't you being a little callous here?"

Of course not. I'm just saying for fifty cents, how much insight do you expect to get from the daily newspaper? If Michael Jordan has a bad night, there's always Scottie Pippen.

"But what about your health?"

Doctors say I can type all I want to.

"Let's talk about burnout. You have been in the league for sixteen years."

That's nothing. My mother taught first grade for over thirty years for a lot less than I'm making and I don't have to convince six-year-olds to sit down and shut up.

"But what about living in the spotlight? Your picture is in the paper. You're a celebrity."

So I'll get a gun.

"You're referring, of course, to Atlanta Falcon receiver Andre Rison, who says he carries a gun because of his celebrity status as a pro football player."

If I were Andre Rison, I would carry two guns. He's not only a celebrity, he also plays for the Falcons.

Lewis on the set of "Designing Women" with Delta Burke and Dixie Carter.

"But don't people often harass you in public for what you write?"

Yo. I don't mind that as long as they don't challenge my manhood.

"Still, there must be other things you would like to

accomplish. As they said about Michael Jordan, there's a lot more to him than just being a great basketball player."

Yeah, like the $46 million in the bank.

"You wouldn't like to, say, go into teaching?"

I can't convince my dog to sit down and shut up.

"How about television?"

Too many have already tried to out-Andy-Rooney Andy Rooney.

"What about acting? You did an episode of 'Designing Women.'"

In one scene I had to hug Delta Burke. Like I said, heavy lifting isn't my bag.

"Some say Michael Jordan is retiring because he's already won three league championships and several most valuable player awards. Is one of the reasons you're not retiring the fact you've never won a Pulitzer?"

Winning the Pulitzer has never entered my mind.

"Oh, come on. The Pulitzer is the highest prize in journalism. Surely you must covet such a prestigious award."

Awards are nice, but I didn't get into the profession to win awards.

"What did you get into it for?"

To get mentioned favorably on the Rush Limbaugh radio show. That was enough for me.

"Michael Jordan retired in his prime. You're telling us you don't think you've reached your prime yet?"

No. I just said I still need a steady job.

"That sounds like a cop out. How much more money do you think you'll need before you feel secure enough to retire?"

Forty-five million and change.

"One more question. What primary goal do you hope to attain before you finally do retire?"

Outlast Beavis and Butt-Head.

"How long might that take?"

November 1996, if we're lucky.

July 1991

Sweet Memories Of The Vine

Thanks to the generosity of a couple of friends, I scored some homegrown (vine ripe, if you please) tomatoes the other day with a street value of at least seven or eight bucks.

You can get these tomatoes only in the summertime, and if you have no garden of your own, you must have a tomato connection.

The rest of the year, one must be content with those tasteless pretenders somebody grows in a hothouse somewhere.

They lack the juice and the flavor of the summertime homegrowns to which, I freely admit, I've become addicted.

I grew up eating homegrown tomatoes from the family garden. It was only after I became an urban creature living far from the tilled soil, I realized what a blessing they had been to me as a child and how dear they are to me now.

Mama would cook green beans with new potatoes and there would be a plate of fresh tomatoes just out of the garden.

The juice from the tomatoes inevitably mixed with the green beans and even got into your corn bread. The mix was indescribably wonderful.

Of course there are other ways to eat homegrown tomatoes. I took one of my friends' offerings last week and sat down and ate it like an apple. Some of the abundant juice ran down my chin onto my shirt like it did with the tomatoes of my youth.

I can still hear Mama: "Look at your shirt, and I just took it off the line."

I get my shirts dry-cleaned now. Oh, for one more of her gentle scoldings.

I also use the tomatoes to make sandwiches. Behold, the fresh homegrown tomato sandwich.

First, you need white bread. Never use any sort of bread other than soft, fresh, white bread — hang the nutritional value — when constructing a tomato sandwich. To use any sort of other bread is a transgression equal to putting lights in Wrigley Field and putting mushrooms on cheeseburgers.

Cover both slices of bread with mayonnaise. Salt and pepper

the slices of tomatoes and then put them between the bread.

Eat quickly. The juice of the tomato slices will soon turn the white bread into mush and you will be wearing some of your tomato sandwich.

My grandfather, Bun Word, sold some of his tomatoes on the side of the road at the little fruit and vegetable stands he ran summers in my hometown of Moreland.

One day he ran out of his own tomatoes and bought some to sell off a produce truck. A couple of Atlanta tourists stopped by.

The lady picked up a basket of tomatoes and asked my grandfather, "Are these homegrown?"

"Yes, ma'am," he said.

She bought a basket of the tomatoes.

I said to my grandfather, "You didn't grow those tomatoes at home."

"Well," he replied, "they were grown at somebody's home."

My grandfather was a God-fearing, foot-washing Baptist, but I later learned it was not considered sinful nor unethical to put the shuck on Atlanta tourists.

In Atlanta they allowed liquor and strippers in various dens of iniquity.

The folks in the hinterlands were just getting even.

My boyhood friend and idol, Weyman C. Wannamaker, Jr., a great American, for instance, once sold cantaloupes to city folk as Exotic Moreland Yellow-meated Midget Watermelons for an obscene profit.

This is just to say be careful if you go out and try to buy homegrown tomatoes. Folks in the country still don't give the rest of us much credit for being very smart. Otherwise, we wouldn't live crammed together like we do and spend half our day fighting traffic and eating, as some do, raw fish.

I've eaten all my tomatoes now and face a rather extensive dry-cleaning bill for the damage they did to my shirts. But it will be a pittance when I consider the ecstasy and memories they provided me.

And to think, it wasn't that long ago I felt the same way about sex.

July 1991

CHAPTER

Seven

"Lewis had a unique gift that let him touch people. He let us know we were not alone... He shared his life experiences and let us find our own parallels. And he always made us laugh. We all felt a kindred spirit in his joy and his pain."

LARRY WHITTINGTON
ALPHARETTA, GEORGIA

Double Shot Of Medallions

Sea Island, Georgia — We had the Swingin' Medallions for a pre-Georgia-Florida football game party here on this lovely isle, home of the five-star retreat, The Cloister.

They come to the Georgia coast by the thousands annually for the game, played in nearby Jacksonville, Florida.

The Swingin' Medallions. I have often asked what, if anything, endures? Well, the Swingin' Medallions and their kind of music — my generation's music — has.

I first heard them sing and play in the parking lot of a fraternity house at the University of Georgia in 1965. They had the land's No. 1 rock 'n' roll hit at the time, the celebrated, "Double Shot of My Baby's Love."

That was so long ago. I'd never been married and my father was living with me. He had appeared at my apartment one day after one of his long absences, hat in hand.

I gave him a bed. He got a job running a local cafeteria. He paid his part of the rent out of what he would bring home to eat each night from the cafeteria. I never had a better eating year.

We were strolling along the campus together and heard the music. We went to the fraternity parking lot from whence it came and listened for a half an hour.

Daddy said, "Marvelous music. Simply marvelous."

My daddy said the same thing about World War II.

"Marvelous war. Simply marvelous."

The major thought practically everything was marvelous, simply marvelous, except women who smoked. I'm not sure why he thought more of world wars than women who smoked. I never got to know the man that well.

The Swingin' Medallions at the party were one original and the sons of originals. How nice to see one generation pass down its music to another. That rarely happens.

What clean-cut, personable young men they were. They let the more celebratory join for a few numbers behind their microphones.

There is something about a microphone and an amplifying system and a little see-through whiskey to bring out imagined musical talent.

They did "Double Shot" twice. And they played all the other great shagging sounds from the '50s and '60s.

Sure, I'll list a few of them: "Stand By Me." Haunting melody if you listen to it very closely. Will you just hang around, darling, even through the bad times?

"My Girl." The Temptations' finest, in my mind.

"Be Young, Be Foolish, Be Happy." The Tams's greatest hit. I know a lady who wants it sung at her funeral.

"It's funny about this kind of music," one of the younger Medallions was saying. "We play for people your age [high side of forty and up] and we play a lot of high school proms.

"The kids like it as much as you do, and they think it's something brand-new."

Compared to what rock 'n' roll became in the '70s, it's tame music, soft music. It is music to which there are actually discernible words.

And, perhaps the best thing about it is, you can actually talk above it.

My generation hasn't given what others have been asked to give.

We've been through no depressions or world wars, for instance. We've given you Bill and Hillary.

But we have left our music, the kind the South Carolina-based Swingin' Medallions still play with great feeling and just the right amount of showmanship for a group that didn't riot when it was announced the bar was closing down at 10:30.

It was a nice party and nobody is young enough to jump in the pool anymore. Marvelous. Simply marvelous.

November 1993

Back On Track

Here's my program for making America economically sane once again:

(1.) Stop all defense spending. Don't buy any more planes, bombs, rifles, bullets, tanks, combat boots or helmets.

Who do we need to defend ourselves from? There's no more Soviet Union, and Canada already has given us hockey, so why would they want to harm us any more? If Saddam Hussein gets cute again, we turn him over to the Israelis, who will not be the nice guys we were and allow Saddam to get out of the Gulf War still above ground.

Savings to the taxpayers: $72 septillion.

(2.) Cut out all welfare. Put everybody who is on welfare to work cleaning up New York city. Put a tax on loud talking and horn blowing in Manhattan to pay for it.

(3.) Do away with the House of Representatives and let each state have just one senator. Make each senator buy his or her own car and build a dormitory for them to sleep in. If anybody tries to raise income taxes or take a junket on taxpayers' expense, we take away his or her mattress in the dorm for a period of time to be determined by a national call-in to "Larry King Live."

Savings to the taxpayers: $43 dodecamillion and a lot of boring speeches.

(4.) Put a tax on sex. At the end of the year, you put down how many times you've had sex, and you're taxed accordingly. Or we could forget that and simply tax Wilt Chamberlain, starting back with his first sexual experience.

Revenue increase: I'm not sure, but another idea is we charge Wilt double for every time he didn't use a condom.

(5.) Make all car dealers who make their own television commercials pay an annoyance-to-the-public fee of $1,000 for each commercial.

Revenue increase: Who cares, if we can get the loudmouths off TV?

(6.) Let the airlines build their own airports and furnish their own flight controllers. If Thomas Jefferson had been asked whether or not he thought the federal government should be in the airport business, he would have answered, "Are you nuts?" Savings to the taxpayers: $727 deltamillion.

(7.) Do away with Amtrak. If there's anything more ridiculous for the federal government to be involved in than airports, it's running a railroad. Let the Walt Disney Co. build one.

Savings to the taxpayers: A billion or so and a lot of time waiting on a train.

(8.) Give the national parks back to the bears. It adds a little more adventure to camping out anyway, knowing there's not a park ranger anywhere within two hundred miles and something large and furry could eat you before morning.

Savings to the taxpayers: I'm not sure, but the concrete tent business would experience a sudden boom.

(9.) Cut out all federal grants, especially for stupid studies like determining how porcupines are able to sleep on their backs. And not a single dime to restore and maintain the homes of famous band leaders, either, especially ones that allowed accordion playing.

Savings to the taxpayers: Enough to buy one helluva lot of champagne.

(10.) Sell the Gadsden Purchase back to Gadsden, whoever that was, and sell Hawaii to the Japanese. They've been trying to take over Hawaii since 1941 and have finally just about succeeded, or at least that's the way it looked to me the last time I was there.

Let's get some money out of the Japanese before they just pick up Hawaii and take it home with them.

Revenue increase: The Japanese probably would give a bundle for Hawaii, and if Gadsden doesn't want to buy his land back, we tell the Japanese it would make a real nice layout for a golf course, and we'll get another bundle.

H. Ross Perot couldn't have said it any better.

April 1992

It's Only Make Believe

A couple of Atlanta television stations this fall decided not to run any political advertisements during the city elections.

Perhaps they figured they give us enough drivel with the lineup of network programming they cast upon us.

Whatever the reason, they are to be commended. Think of what we were spared: "My opponent wears smelly socks, kidnaps little puppies and eats raw wienies."

"That's nothing. My opponent sucks eggs, runs rabbits and doesn't close his eyes during prayer."

"You think that's disgusting. The idiot running against me has a wart on his nose, supports thespianism and sold Kool-Aid to Jim Jones."

If only television stations could be convinced to become more discerning toward all sorts of commercials, not just those of a political nature, as has been the case in Atlanta.

I made a list of the sort of television commercials I despise the most, and in a perfect world I would never have to see them again.

Here is my list:

AUTOMOBILE COMMERCIALS. "Hey, we're giving these cars away! No, we'll pay you to take them off our hands!" I actually come from a long line of used-car dealers and horse thieves, but local car dealers have no business doing their own commercials on television. They are loud, they are obnoxious and they kidnap little puppies. Call BR 549 if you agree.

CEREAL COMMERCIALS. There simply can't be that much difference among cereals. Muleslick, or whatever it's called, can't be any better friend to your colon than Bowel Bran. Can it? Of course it can't. And, furthermore, I don't care if cereal becomes soggy, that's why I put milk in it. Bowel Bran today. Can Tree Bark be far behind?

FEMININE HYGIENE PRODUCTS. I'll keep this simple and discreet. I don't care if it will hold and absorb the entire

Atlantic Ocean, I don't want to have to sit in my den and hear about it on my television.

DIARRHEA AND CONSTIPATION COMMERCIALS. This family goes to Hawaii and they all come down with diarrhea and can't get out of their room. It happens. But I don't care. Just pretend you're doing the hula and find a facility.

PERFUME AND COLOGNE COMMERCIALS. I could abide these if they made any sense. But they rarely do. There's a naked couple, except for sunglasses, riding orangutans through a field of nuclear waste, and it's a commercial about a new cologne named "Goat Sweat."

A man likes to smell like a man. A woman like a woman. Not a bodily function or the scent of the North Dakota female doodlebug in heat.

LAWYER COMMERCIALS. Every ambulance chaser in the country has his or her own television commercial. "The law firm of Loophole and Whiplash will sue anybody, living or dead, for the low, low price of $29.95.

"Judge Wapner is our first cousin, by the way, and we've read all the John Grisham novels. Trust us."

Yeah, and those law books behind you were painted on the walls. Go for a court-appointed attorney and hope he or she doesn't stutter.

PET FOOD COMMERCIALS. "This dog food is beefy and chewy tasting."

How does the announcer know that? The dog didn't tell him.

HAIR COMMERCIALS. If God hadn't wanted you to be bald, you'd have been born with a cat on your head.

Get rid of insurance commercials featuring aging actors, and stop telling me that Juan Valdez is from Colombia and we're supposed to believe he's got coffee in those sacks.

So many bad commercials. So little space.

November 1993

Economists Take Note

Some might scoff at the fact I consider myself quite the expert on the economy.

I am not without portfolio. I was treasurer of my freshman class in high school and I take the *Wall Street Journal* at home.

I don't read it, but when friends drop by, they are impressed when they see my dog, Catfish, eating table scraps off the front page.

We've been hearing about certain economic indicators lately, and economists look at things like housing starts, retail sales and the hemlines of women's dresses to predict what's forthcoming for the economy.

Over the years I have developed my own set of economic indicators and they have proven to be trustworthy.

I was able to predict the stock market crash of a few years ago.

A couple of days before the fall I tried to get in touch with my broker and got a recording saying his phone had been disconnected.

I knew that was a sure sign the bottom was about to fall out on the Amalgamated Goat and International Mushrooms he had sold me a couple of days earlier and I told all my friends, "Get out of the market."

They didn't listen, however, and a number of them now live in cardboard boxes.

What follows is a list of the indicators I use to tell me exactly what state the economy is in:

Golf tees: If you play golf, notice how many perfectly good tees have been left on tee boxes. If there are lots of them, then the economy is fine.

People are in such good shape financially they don't even bother to bend over and pluck their tees out of the ground after they've hit.

If there are no tees left, it means people are tightening their belts and you might want to show up for work one day next week instead of lollygagging around on the golf course.

Deion Sanders: If his monthly bill for jewelry drops under $100,000, tough times are ahead.

Roach Motel: If you notice yours has a lot of vacancies each time you check it, even the roaches are feeling the crunch and staying home more.

Tipping: If you leave your waiter a lousy tip and he not only complains, he also attempts to pistol-whip you, it's a sign you should be at home eating fish sticks instead of being out at a fancy restaurant.

Ex-wives: If more than one calls in a single day to complain about the amount of alimony you're paying them, you can bet that luxury items such as Gucci pocketbooks and the silky things they wear at night for their boyfriends have gone sky-high.

Jesse Jackson: If a crisis breaks out somewhere and Jesse's not right in the middle of it making speeches, it means whoever picks up the tab to send him all over the world has decided to cut back.

My dog, Catfish, incidentally, thinks the economy is in sad shape.

He's been eating off copies of old campaign literature lately.

My subscription to the *Wall Street Journal* ran out and I was afraid to re-up. Jesse hasn't been in the Middle East in weeks now.

November 1990

The Buzz In Moreland

Now here's my little hometown of Moreland, forty miles south and fifty years from Atlanta. It is still a village of maybe four hundred, and it still doesn't have a traffic light and it doesn't want one.

Oh, there's been a little progress since I left dear Moreland nearly thirty years ago.

There's a new brick post office, for instance, that succeeds the old wooden one.

Somebody even built a couple of tennis courts in Moreland and there actually is a Moreland exit sign on Interstate 85, which missed my hometown by three miles to the north.

Still, after all these years, Moreland has remained a quiet little blip on the map, a haven for those who have no use for city lights.

So you can imagine just how shocked I was after reading a letter I received from Alan E. Thomas, who works in Atlanta.

Alan E. Thomas wrote to tell me that he and his wife have spent the last three years constructing a new farm home in Moreland.

"Like so many others," he wrote, "we're leaving city life and beginning to experience the wonders of the country.

"At night we can step out on the deck and actually see stars again and hear the crickets, frogs and whippoorwills and spot herds of deer crossing from one tree cluster to another."

Ah, such splendor. Such peace.

But Alan E. Thomas and his wife and other Moreland citizens suddenly are faced with a problem I never thought could happen there.

Jet noise.

I can recall the noise of freight trains rumbling through Moreland nights during my childhood, and once a local turkey farmer got upset because he said the Baptist church's chimes made his turkeys nervous. But jet noise? Alan E. Thomas writes that the Coweta County Airport Authority wants to expand its little facility, which sits just on the out-skirts of Moreland, so it can accommodate corporate jets. Corporate jets? I doubt any corporate jets would land there to do any business in Moreland. There is the expanding county seat of Newnan nearby, but any corporate jets with business in Newnan simply could land at Hartsfield.

It's only twenty-five miles away.

Alan E. Thomas wants to be able to continue hearing the rural night sounds and not have them drowned out by the menacing roar of a jet engine.

He and others have suggested a new airport be built some-where else.

But the airport authority has explained that the Federal Aviation Administration will grant funds for a runway extension but not for a completely new airport.

Governmental red tape and bureaucratic bumfuzzle strikes again.

Mr. Thomas has suggested I become an ally in the fight against jet noise in Moreland, and I assure him he now can count me on his side.

Moreland and Newnan need a place for jets to take off and land like they need a subway station, and rural nights should still belong to the crickets, frogs and whippoorwills.

Fight like hell, my fellow Morelanders, and save the sacred quiet.

Once that's lost, God forbid, a traffic light is sure to follow.

December 1990

CHAPTER

Eight

"When he wrote serious things, it would just tear your heart out."

JOYCE MADDOX
LOVEJOY, GEORGIA

No Yogurt Allowed
In Smoky Cafe

Somewhere in Kentucky — It was a truck stop. The sign in front didn't say it was a truck stop, but it was a truck stop.

The fact there were a lot of trucks parked outside was my first clue. My second was that inside the restaurant there sat a lot of men wearing caps, smoking cigarettes and drinking coffee.

Truck drivers will, in fact, wear caps, smoke cigarettes and drink coffee.

It was raining. I was trying to get from Lexington to Memphis.

To travel by air between those two cities you have to connect through Cincinnati. Or maybe it was Salt Lake City.

It was lunch time. Eat right, say the lifestyle police, or you die.

OK, I'll have the steamed vegetable plate, bottled water and yogurt for dessert so I can live to be a 112-year-old Russian.

The waitress's name was Irene. She was pleasant.

"What's it going to be, Hon?" she asked me.

To be honest, there weren't many choices. There was no steamed vegetable plate or bottled water or yogurt on the menu.

About the only thing that wasn't fried was the iced tea. I suppose liver and onions was the healthiest choice, but I ordered the chopped sirloin. I don't eat raw fish, steamed vegetables or liver.

A chopped sirloin steak once was known as a hamburger steak. I saw a huge neon sign in Nashville recently advertising "pre-owned vehicles." They were once known as used cars.

Irene brought my chopped sirloin. It had a fried onion ring on top. I also had French fried potatoes and two white bread rolls, like you used to get all the time before it was decided white bread would send you to an early grave.

"Hope you enjoy it, Hon," said Irene.

I did. The last time I had a hamburger steak this greasy and good was at Steve Smith's Truck Stop back home in Moreland.

It cost $1.25. This was only $4.95 over thirty years later.

As I ate I looked around. Randy Travis was playing on the jukebox.

There were several families wearing the colors of a high school football team they were on their way to see play in the state finals in Louisville.

Some of the families were black. Others were white. The waitresses had pushed several tables together so they could eat as a group.

The mothers, I noticed, actually were allowing their children to eat those white rolls.

The truck driver sitting nearest to me was smoking an unfiltered Camel cigarette between bites of liver and onions.

I left Irene a little extra for her pleasantness and then went to the register. A rather stout young woman stood behind it.

"Evuh thang aw-rite?" she asked me. Peterbilts don't rumble that low when they are cranked on cold mornings.

"It was fine," I said to her, realizing I wouldn't have dared tell her otherwise if it hadn't been. She took my money and then she gave me my change.

"Now you keep the rough side off the pavement and let the smooth side slide," is what she said to me as I walked out.

Later, after I had time to think about it, I decided that is truck talk for, "Don't sweat the small stuff."

Fearing for my life, I only ate one of those two white rolls. If I had it to do over again, I would have eaten them both.

December 1993

A Case Of Jack Daniels, Please

It's time somebody stood up and defended Christopher Columbus, who wasn't trying to do anybody any harm when he discovered the New World five hundred years ago.

Chris was just inquisitive, and he wasn't going for any of that business about the world being flat.

Chris was always saying to his friends, "If the world is flat and there is no New World out there somewhere, I'll eat my hat."

And Christopher Columbus, in renderings I have seen, usually was wearing a large hat with some feathers on it.

It's one thing to eat a baseball cap or a beret, but try to get a large hat with feathers on it down the hatch and you've got quite the gastronomical dilemma on your hands. Columbus had a lot of risk here.

And somebody finally took him up on his bet.

He said, "OK, Mr. Know-It-All, why don't we get three ships and start sailing out to sea? If we come to the end of the Earth, we can turn around and sail back and we'll watch you eat that goofy hat of yours.

"But if we find out the world is round and there's a New World out there like you say there is, I'll eat your hat and come over to your house on Saturday mornings for a month and wax your car."

Columbus replied, "It's 1492. We don't have cars."

"OK," said his challenger, "then I'll wax your horse."

Columbus couldn't back down. But he had a problem. He didn't have the money for the three ships.

So he went to Queen Isabella.

"I'll give you the money for your three ships," the queen said to Columbus, "but if you do find the world is round and there is a New World, I want you to bring me back a hair dryer, a Lady Schick electric razor, a case of Jack Daniels and some shag carpet."

Columbus agreed. He bought three ships with the money

Queen Isabella gave him and named them Nina, Pinta and Santa Maria for the original Shirelles, who got their start in Europe in the late 1400s, as did Columbus.

So off Columbus went. There was a lot of scurvy and rickets during the trip, but the world turned out to be round just like Columbus said it was.

He landed in the New World, bought a condo on an ocean-front golf development, picked up everything Queen Isabella wanted and sailed home.

His challenger did, in fact, eat Columbus's hat. Unfortunately, it was the only hat Columbus had and, being unable to keep his head warm, the brave explorer caught pneumonia, died and was never able to return to live in his condo or see Disney World.

He did, however, leave the shiniest horse in town.

But it's politically correct now to blame Columbus for what was to come later, a mass exodus of people from the Old World to the New World, which led to New York City, congresspersons, smog, Miami Beach, shopping malls, various diseases and the disappearance of the snail darter.

The popular phrase now is, "Columbus didn't discover America, he conquered it."

Listen, somebody else would have done it sooner or later. Humans have always sought new horizons.

And we're still doing it five hundred years later. What about all those astronauts we sent into outer space? We look upon them as heroes, but there are those who want to defame Christopher Columbus.

Did any of our astronauts have to deal with scurvy or rickets? Did any of them have to raise their own money to pay for the trip? No.

I say hats off to Columbus. It's like Queen Isabella said when he delivered the hair dryer, the Lady Schick razor, the booze and the carpet: "Chris, you da man."

October 1992

Zapping The Silly Sports

Someone once wrote the only uncomfortable thing that lasts longer than the National Basketball Association season is pregnancy.

One could say the same for that silly sport of hockey. They puck it up and down the ice for what seems like an entire year until a bunch of guys with names out of a Victor Hugo novel and no teeth skate around with Stanley's Cup.

They play pro basketball for six months in order to eliminate Sacramento and then they start over and play until the Fourth of July.

With no Michael Jordan in the league anymore, they might as well call the whole thing off anyway.

Wouldn't bother me. The last time anybody was able to get me to a pro basketball game, Kareem Abdul-Jabbar was a tall guy named Lew.

But now they're doing the same thing to the baseball season. I love baseball. I've always loved baseball.

And baseball used to make absolutely perfect sense. There were two leagues, the National and the American. At the end of a 154-game season, the winners of the two leagues played in the World Series. In the daytime. On real grass. Under the sky, not a roof named for it.

And each team in each league could use only nine players at a time.

Then somebody said in the American League there could be something called a designated hitter.

The pitcher on each team — pitchers are notoriously poor hitters for some reason — could stay in the dugout when it came his time to bat and somebody else could go up there and hit for him.

Why God hasn't intervened for that transgression is still a mystery. God got even with North Carolina for putting slaw on barbecue. He (or She; excuse, please) did. He or She sent North Carolina good ol' Jesse Helms.

But they still weren't through messing with baseball. They

also split each league into two divisions. Gave away franchises in foreign countries, allowed artificial grass, put roofs on stadiums and started playing the World Series in the middle of the night on the brink of November.

They still weren't finished. Beginning next season, each league will be split into three divisions and there will be another round of playoffs.

You play 162 games from April until October and the issue of the best team in each league still isn't settled without two rounds of playoffs.

The federal government couldn't screw up baseball any worse than baseball has screwed up baseball, and I mean that as the insult that it most certainly is.

Baseball is a pure game, an orderly game. The reason the uneducated think it's a dull, slow game is they don't realize the intricacies involved in every pitch.

"A lot of stuff goes on out there" is how it was described in George Will's baseball book, *Men at Work*.

But now there is an obvious move afoot to junk-up baseball.

"We're modernizing it is all," say those behind the changes. Money-izing is what they're doing. More playoff games mean more money.

Can't there be anything left in this world that isn't given power steering, an automatic timer, doesn't do your thinking for you, or isn't diluted for quick cash? I liked hotels better when they had big brass keys, not a plastic card to get inside your room.

I liked country music better before there were guitars you plugged in. I liked bacon better when I could hear it sizzling in a pan and smell it frying. That was before you could zap it in a microwave.

Now, baseball will be like basketball and hockey. It will last much too long, give too many also-rans a second, undeserved chance and Port-au-Prince will probably get a team and somebody will shoot Jeff Blauser of the Braves, my favorite baseball player, one night.

The Nightmare Before Christmas. Soon, that might describe the baseball season.

October 1993

Put It Back On, Madonna

It used to be you really had to search to find anything that resembled smut.

I saw my first official smut in the sixth grade when a classmate came to school with a deck of cards that featured black and white photographs of men and women having sex with one another.

The classmate's older brother had come home on leave from the Navy and had brought the cards with him.

A group of us went down behind the collapsing grandstand of the school baseball field and passed around the cards.

"Why do these people have black bars across their faces?" Alvin Bates, the class nerd, asked.

"So their mothers won't recognize them," somebody answered.

Other than the cards, all that was available to titillate was a calendar with a girl in a bikini on it down at the service station and the women's underwear section of the Sears & Roebuck catalog.

Even when *Playboy* came along, you didn't get to see it all. I think it was better that way. When you did find something of an explicit nature you appreciated it a great deal.

Today, smut is everywhere. There's *Playboy*, which finally was forced to show it all in order to remain competitive with other such publications as *Penthouse*, *High Society* and *Hustler*.

Sexually explicit movies of the X-rated variety are available in your living room on cable, and you can go down to your local video store and rent everything from *Deep Throat* to *Debbie Does the Entire Southwest Portion of the United States, including the Gadsden Purchase.*

I bring up all this as a means of asking what's the big deal about Madonna's book, *Sex*, which from what I've been hearing on the news includes photographs of this woman acting out her sexual fantasies.

They're getting $50 for this book and it's a runaway best-seller. I could understand this, perhaps, if it were 1958 and your older brother had to come home from the Navy before you could see any raunch.

But fifty bucks in this day and time to see Madonna naked and strapped to the hood of a 1971 Cadillac to act out her desire to be a hood ornament? Come on. In the first place, Madonna isn't exactly a goddess. Kim Basinger naked and strapped to the hood of a 1971 Cadillac might be worth a few bucks to see, but not Madonna.

Meryl Streep is better-looking than Madonna, and Meryl Streep would have a hard time finishing third in the annual Collard Festival Beauty Contest in Lard Bucket, Alabama.

In the second place, can't everybody see the scam here? The publisher seals the book like what's inside are state secrets or the formula for Coca-Cola and then sets the price at half a hundred to indicate further what's between the covers is the dangest thing since soap.

Frankly, I don't care what Madonna's sexual fantasies are. I've already seen her strutting around on television singing in her underwear. The only thing about Madonna and *Sex* I'm interested in is what would her mother think about all this? That's her little girl. In her worst nightmares did she ever think her little girl would grow up as a smut peddler and wouldn't have the decency to at least cover her face with a black bar?

Sex. That starts with *S* and that stands for Sucker. I'll just wait for the next Victoria's Secret catalog.

February 1993

Here's The Beef

In protest for what I consider to be recent unfair attacks on beef, one of my favorite meats, I went out and had myself a thick, juicy T-bone at Longhorn Steaks the other night.

It was great, as usual. I would have eaten two if my stomach would have held another because we beef-eaters need to do all we can to tell the wimps and weenies who have put themselves in charge of our lifestyles to go eat a bucket of worms (a.k.a. sushi).

It's cow meat they're after now. One group says we're being cruel by killing cows and chopping them into steaks.

There's a book out about the evils, both social and physical, of eating beef as well. I refuse to name it here and give it any publicity.

And then I read a story in the papers about a report from the American Chemical Society saying the natural substance that gives beef its meaty taste has been synthesized in the laboratory and may be used to turn tofu into a substitute for beef.

Do what? I asked a health nut to tell me what tofu is. It sounds to me like a ballet dance step.

"It's soybean-based," she explained.

So let me see if I have this straight.

Some scientist has come up with something in his lab to put in something made out of soybeans, and I'm supposed to eat that instead of beef? The magic ingredient is BMP. Said the article, "BMP could be used to make imitation beef with little or no saturated fat similar to the way fake crab meat is made."

Fake crab meat? What's going on here?

In the first place, I once ate a soybean burger. Another friend of mine, also a health nut, said, "Try this, you might like it."

Somebody once said the same thing to me about marriage.

The soybean burger was awful, so I went to Wendy's and got myself a double with cheese to get the taste out of my mouth.

In the second place, when are those self-appointed jerks going to stop jacking us around about our food? Remember when you were growing up how important it was to eat eggs? "Eat the rest of those eggs, young man," my mother would say, "so you'll grow up big and strong."

Not anymore. Now they say eggs cause diphtheria, not to mention shortness and weakness, so somebody has come out with a fake egg.

I bet a chicken could tell the difference.

Pork has been put down as unhealthy. Some chickens have tumors in them and fish have mercury, and I never knew there was such a thing as fake crab meat until now.

So what's left to eat? Nothing much. If what we read and hear is true, we'd all be better off if we didn't eat anything at all, never had sex, abstained from drinking, smoking and gambling, and died on the operating table instead of getting a blood transfusion that could give us AIDS.

Life used to be fun. Now it's just one big Don't.

But I'll tell you what I'm going to do. I'm going to continue to eat beef and everything else I like. I will never walk into a Longhorn and say, "I'll have the tofu T-bone, please."

If doing such a thing kills me, it'll just have to kill me.

I think I'd rather go suddenly from a beef overdose than live long enough to get really sick and wind up croaking in a hospital bed where they've been keeping me alive by feeding me through a tube.

There should be the basic right to live free from as much worry as possible. But how can you, when not a day passes that we aren't told what's the latest thing that's bad for us? Eat, drink and be merry, I say, for tomorrow you may choke on a big piece of broccoli.

April 1992

CHAPTER

"As a native Southerner who for five years has been living in Chicago, 'in exile,' as Lewis once so aptly put it, I'm grieving long-distance for the loss of a dear friend. Somewhere, dogwoods and azaleas still bloom in the spring and folks still talk to their neighbors."

NEVA HILLIARD
BENSENVILLE, ILLINOIS

The Tight Twosome

Great Waters, Georgia — My dog Catfish, the black Lab, took to the water here at lovely Lake Oconee as he did to steak bones.

Knowing the history and heritage of the black Lab, I obviously didn't expect anything different. This type of dog makes a marvelous retriever of recently shot fowl that fall dead into water.

I do not take part in shooting at birds who happen to be flying over water, despite the fact I have a black Lab, but the first time I tossed a stick into Lake Oconee from the shore near my home, Catfish dutifully jumped in and retrieved it.

Catfish has go-get-the-stick down perfectly. He hasn't learned give-back-the-stick, however. I suppose even if I did down a bird with my trusty shotgun he would figure the late prey belonged to him, since he was the one who went to all the trouble to bring it to shore, and he wouldn't turn it over to me for dinner.

I'm still in a recovery period from heart surgery in March and I walk each day. I walk down by the lake and Catfish always goes with me.

As we walk, I usually toss a stick or two into the water for him to retrieve. I can't throw it very far with a sternum that's still not completely anchored back in place after being halved for my surgery. I could throw my fast ball in a school zone and still not be over the speed limit.

So the stick goes only forty or fifty feet into the water, barely past wading distance. That's as far as I'd ever seen Catfish go out into the lake.

Catfish and I were on one of our daily walks this week when he espied a gaggle of adult and baby geese a few feet off shore.

The geese had gotten his attention before but since they hadn't been shot, I guess he didn't think he was supposed to attempt to retrieve them.

But this time, something snapped in my dog. He dove into the water and swam after the geese. The geese commenced individual honking fits and swam outward into the lake.

Catfish followed them.

The geese kept swimming toward the middle of the lake and so did Catfish, in a heated aquatic pursuit.

I suddenly could no longer see my dog. I could barely see the geese, they were so far out into the lake. Where was my dog? Unsettling thoughts began to enter my mind.

I knew black Labs were great swimmers, but certainly they couldn't just swim forever. Did dogs know there is a limit to how far and how long they can swim and still get safely back to shore? Had Catfish already slipped under the water and drowned? Would I be the first person ever to have a black Lab drown? I felt completely helpless. Naturally, I cried out for him, recalling the words of a friend who once said, "Ever notice that dogs and children never listen once they're outside?" There was nobody else around. I had no boat, and I certainly couldn't swim out to save my dog.

Finally, I saw Catfish's head emerge perhaps 150 yards out. He wasn't about to catch a goose because as soon as he would get near one, it simply would flap its wings and move several more feet away from him.

The problem was, he didn't know that.

Catfish started toward the shore and I was greatly relieved. Then a goose honked to his right and he was back out into the lake after it. I'm not sure how long my dog had been in the water to that point, but I was getting close to a panic.

Catfish eventually gave up on the geese and swam back to shore. It seemed to take him an eternity to make it the last fifty yards, but he was safe and hardly seemed winded.

And ever notice how a dog must be in licking distance of a human being before it can shake itself dry? But I didn't mind getting wet. I felt a little like an idiot for thinking one of the great breeds of water dogs would be stupid enough to swim out into a lake after a gaggle of geese so far it couldn't make it back, but Catfish and I are a rather tight twosome, and getting sprayed with half Lake Oconee off his coat was no bother as long as I had him next to me again.

Now, I want parents of small children to read this again. Summer's here. The water beckons. Keep an eye on those little darlings.

Unfortunately, they don't know nearly as much about their limits and pools, ponds and lakes as dogs do.

June 1993

Lazing With Little Debbie

I've been working a lot harder since the Japanese prime minister said Americans are lazy.

Here I am laboring now, for instance. I'd rather be on the golf course or in front of my television watching a movie and feeding my face with Little Debbie Snack Cakes.

Actually, I'd rather be out with Little Debbie, who's probably grown by now and has even better snack cakes.

But it's time we showed the Japanese a thing or two about just how hard Americans will work once they are challenged.

Yesterday I made up my bed before it really needed making up.

Usually I don't make up my bed until it no longer resembles a bed, but is stacked with dirty clothes, magazines I've been reading in the bed, Little Debbie Snack Cake wrappers and an occasional shoe.

At that point it looks more like a sidewalk in New York City than a bed, and I know it's time to make it up.

But I went ahead and picked up all the garbage on my bed and swept off the sheets and pillows before I really needed to.

I didn't spot one single thing that was alive, as a matter of fact.

Often there are organisms in there somewhere, including things I had to catch and mount for my tenth-grade biology bug collection.

"Take that, Mr. Prime Minister," I said as I swept the last graham cracker crumb off the bed. I'd run out of Little Debbie Snack Cakes one recent evening and had to go to graham crackers.

After that, I looked around for something else to do to show Mr. Prime Minister he couldn't call me lazy and get away with it.

I put my dishes, the ones that were still in the sink following my Annual Ground Hog Day party, in the dishwasher.

I'm probably the only person who has an Annual Ground

Hog Day party. I invite guests and we eat and drink and then go outside to see if we can see our shadows. If we do, it means I don't clean up the dishes from the party for six weeks. If we don't, it means I don't clean up the dishes from the party for six more weeks.

But here I was doing my duty as an American, putting the dishes in the dishwasher a good two weeks before I really had to.

Talk about living things. I think there was a cat in there among those dishes, because once I put them in the dishwasher and cut it on, there emanated a loud noise that sounded a lot like a cat having just been scalded by hot, soapy water.

When I empty the dishwasher sometime around Flag Day in June, I suppose I'll find out exactly what was making that noise.

Then I decided to clean out my bedroom closet.

I removed a large pile of items that included clothes I no longer wear, like my polyester leisure suits I had thrown in there during the '70s, an empty jar of mayonnaise, some auto parts, assorted empty beer cans, an autographed picture of Jimmy Swaggart and my dog, Catfish, the black Lab.

"So this is where you've been," I said to Catfish, who had been missing for a couple of weeks. I suppose he had gone into the closet looking for a cat, got trapped under all that stuff and subsisted on mayonnaise until I finally freed him.

After all that work, I was ready for a nap. I dreamt the Japanese prime minister got arrested for loitering.

March 1992

You Can't Fool
Grandmother Nature

My grandmother, Willie Word, noticed it way back in the 1960s when the United States and the Soviet Union were trying to see who could launch the most gadgets into outer space.

"The weather sure has been funny lately," my Uncle Dorsey said as we sat on the porch one hot Sunday afternoon in February.

"It's them satellites," Mama Willie said. "They've messed up the world bad."

I put no stock in this. It was exciting to me to watch those launches and see men ride around in outer space, and if the weather got a little squirrelly occasionally, that was not much to give up to win the space race against the Russians.

Somebody at school had mentioned that if the Soviets beat us to the moon, it would be easier for them to bomb us, so it was really my patriotic duty to pull hard for the red, white and blue in the heavens to avoid being nuked.

We eventually won the race to the moon, of course. I saw the landing on my television.

Mama Willie was pretty skeptical about that, too. "It looked fake to me," she said.

This is the same woman who thought the professional wrestling she saw on television on Saturday afternoons was the real thing. All that, I suppose, is in the eyes of the beholder.

But the last several years, I've been noticing the weather is acting a little strangely myself. There was something like a tidal wave that hit Daytona Beach, Fla., not long ago.

I nearly bought the farm in a tornado a few weeks ago. I thought tornadoes came in the springtime.

Hurricanes seem to be getting even more ferocious. And did you see what happened in New York City over the weekend? A storm hit and it rained so hard and for so long, it swamped cars on FDR Drive, flooded La Guardia Airport and closed down the subway.

Ninety-mph winds were recorded in December in New

York. It's supposed to snow in New York in December. Anybody who has seen *Miracle On 34th Street*, as I have a thousand times, knows that.

Of course, all sorts of other changes are taking place regarding the elements. There's global warming and droughts and the holes in the ozone layer.

And let us not forget the Atlanta Braves have won back-to-back National League pennants. I know that doesn't have anything to do with the weather, but it was still an odd occurrence.

I'm beginning to think Mama Willie might have been right about those satellites.

Later, she even found a quotation from the Bible she said backed her up. I'm not certain which book carried the quotation, but it likely came from Revelation, where there's all that other spooky stuff about the moon turning to blood and locusts the size of Shetland ponies eating people.

Mama Willie, whom I loved dearly, didn't live long enough to see what all else has happened in space. She missed shuttle missions and all the talk about Star Wars.

But she would have been suspect of it all, and she left me that legacy.

And, for the record, I think Kris Kringle was who he said he was in *Miracle on 34th Street*, and New York City needed a good flushing out.

December 1992

It's All Downhill From Here, Olaf

It's time again for my semi-occasional anti-snow-skiing column.

This column began eight years ago on top of a mountain in Vail, Colorado.

Get the picture? The windchill factor is twice my age. My feet hurt because they are in ski boots. They don't make ski boots that don't hurt your feet. That's why all skiers are red in the face. Their feet are killing them.

I am tired. I am angry. I am tired and angry because I am on top of a mountain in Vail in the dead of winter and my feet hurt and my face is red.

A friend is with me. He didn't have to say this, but he did: "Do you realize," he said to me, "we could be in Florida playing golf?" But no, we're on top of this stupid mountain, which presented another problem. We had to get down it on skis.

I said to God, "God, if you'll get me down off this mountain and out of these ski boots and into a hot shower, I'll never ski again."

Like God really cared if I really skied again. Maybe God did care.

If God had intended us to snow ski, God would have never given us a bar with a fireplace in it.

My friend and I got down off the mountain. Neither one of us ever skied again. Thanks, God.

The reason for this semi-occasional anti-snow-skiing column is the Winter Olympics are going on. They're skiing up a storm at the Games in Lillehammer.

I watch them ski on TV and remember when I used to ski. I write another anti-snow-skiing column. That's how big-time journalism works.

Seriously, I tried to become a snow skier despite the fact God — that name again — made me a sun person and allowed me to live in the sunny South.

A number of my Atlanta friends began going West to ski. They said to me, "Come on out. Once you learn to ski it's a lot of fun."

Lewis gracefully negotiates another Vail slope.

They lied.

I learned to ski. It was no fun. I had to take $40,000 worth of ski lessons from some guy in tight pants named Olaf.

Skiing, as a matter of fact, was easy to learn. All you do to ski is aim your skis downhill and take off. You'll ski.

Teaching me to stop and turn going downhill on skis is what made Olaf the rich man he is today.

If you've never skied before and are thinking of trying, just remember the following: It's expensive. You have to travel to a ski area, buy a new wardrobe, rent a bunch of gear, buy a lift ticket, pay Olaf for lessons and pay for four nights in a condo. You can bribe an Atlanta politician for less than it costs for one ski trip.

You can get hurt — and not just your feet. I fell getting off the lift and a chair hit me in the back of the head. The only time my feet didn't hurt was the thirty minutes I was unconscious.

Forget the nightlife. You'll be too sore and tired.

Anybody who would go somewhere cold in the winter is an idiot.

I can say that I was one of those idiots, but a religious experience saved me. I'd send money to Oral Roberts, but I still owe Olaf two more payments.

February 1994

Goodbye, Old Soldiers

It's happened to me before, running into men who served with my late father in World War II.

This time I was in Greensboro, North Carolina, at a bookstore. I was signing copies of one of mine.

I noticed the old man at the first of the hour. He stood at the entrance of the store, looking at me.

After the hour, the signing was over. Meekly, the man walked to where I was sitting.

He had one of those faces that said, here's somebody's beloved grandfather. There was a lot of knowledge and caring in it.

Without another word, he said, "Your daddy was my first sergeant in World War II."

I've studied my father's record as a soldier closely and I know he was in France, then in Germany, and I know he later was sent back to Korea.

"He saved my life in Germany," the man continued. "He saved a lot of lives, and they gave him a battlefield commission."

According to a copy of the citation I have, the colonel had been killed and the unit was under heavy German fire. Sergeant Grizzard reorganized the company, running in the open where the bullets flew, and saved himself and his men from certain annihilation.

"If it weren't for your daddy," the man said, "I wouldn't be here today."

How do you respond to something like that? I certainly was proud of my father at that moment — to think this man had carried for half a century the memories of what my father did that day. And to think he would come to me after all this time. It was like he was trying to thank me for something my father did fifty years ago.

I think I managed a "Bless you," or a "Thanks for looking me up."

We shook hands and the old man walked away. My eyes teared as he did.

My parents' generation, I sincerely believe, had more to bear than any other in this country's history. Their lives were affected — and some were ruined — by World War I, the Great Depression, World War II and Korea, and some lost children in Vietnam. And now the last of them are fading into the shadows cast by the young they brought into this world.

A national magazine, noting the passing of the presidency to someone too young to have had the World War II experience, offered a spread titled, "Goodbye, Old Soldier."

George Bush was the youngest fighter pilot in the Navy during World War II. Now he has gone to his retirement, having been replaced by one with no military experience whatsoever, one whose dealings with the draft system still leave a number of unanswered questions.

The Old Soldiers have moved out, and the Baby Boomers have moved in. That is unsettling to me. The country's leadership, save a few veteran members of Congress, is in the hands of those never tested by fire.

Few of my generation really know the meaning of sacrifice. What did we ever want for and couldn't have? When have we ever been hungry? When did most of us ever have to run through a hail of bullets in a foreign land in order to save comrades? I never have and neither has Bill Clinton.

After the man in Greensboro had walked away, I realized I had made a mistake by not sitting with him and asking him to tell me what happened that day in Germany. I would have liked to have known about it from a survivor, not from some document.

But you know how it is. We're all in a hurry. We just don't know where it is we're hurrying to.

Goodbye, Old Soldiers, and thank you.

You are the very best of us.

August 1993

CHAPTER

Ten

*"I discovered Lewis Grizzard in the
summer of '88, a particularly lonesome
time for me. I could read through the
laughs that he was lonely, too. Thank
God I'm no longer alone. I'll need somebody to help me cope with the loss of
my funny and lonely friend."*

JUDITH SMITH
BAKERSFIELD, CALIFORNIA

Old Men, Boys And The Iron Horse

Aboard the Coast Starlight — What surprises me is that during all this congressional fighting regarding Bill Clinton's budget, there hasn't been a large surge against Amtrak.

Before each budget is passed, at least a few members of Congress usually scream about the government operating a "stage coach system in the jet age" and want to cut off Amtrak's funds.

Amtrak is an easy target. Not many people depend on passenger trains anymore, especially outside the Washington-Boston corridor.

And members of Congress have those big expense accounts anyway so they can fly, and the president has his own jet, big enough to haul Hillary, Chelsea, the cat and whomever else might need a haircut.

But some of us still enjoy a train ride occasionally, and I had the occasion to ride this train, the Coast Starlight, between Seattle and Oakland.

I wanted to see what Washington and Oregon looked like. I had seen them from 35,000 feet, but the world looks a lot alike from that distance. I've flown over Moscow and Montgomery, Alabama, for instance. It would be hard to tell the difference from 35,000 feet, believe it or not.

I booked a bedroom for the twenty-four-hour trip. The bed was comfortable. I had a bathroom. There was even a shower in it. There was a large window and when we stopped at Portland, a machine washed it so I could see the scenery better.

At the station in Seattle they made an announcement for passengers to watch our personal belongings because pickpockets had been lurking there.

I'm certain pickpockets also lurk in airports, and I thought it was nice for Amtrak to warn us. I put my wallet in my front pocket and sat on my bag. Nobody got either one of them.

A word about the shower in my room on the train: The idea was to sit on the toilet seat and then use the little hose on the wall to shower. It was like trying to take a shower in a bud vase. Bending over was out of the question. I concentrated on my underarms.

I had a cheeseburger for lunch. A lady sitting across from me, who said she was a college professor, ordered a chicken concoction with sauce on it that she didn't like. When you're on a train or in a place where there's a cop acting as a maitre d', keep it simple and always order the cheeseburger.

I passed on the fish and had a fairly good steak for dinner. I had scrambled eggs for breakfast as we arrived in Oakland. The train station in Oakland is a death wish and the pick-pockets probably have smelly underarms.

The scenery on the train was stunning. We ran over a spotted owl in Washington, but it was an accident.

The Cascade mountains of Oregon took my breath. There were lakes with old men and boys fishing in them, and nearly all looked up long enough to wave to the train. A wise man once said, "As long as there are trains, there will be old men and boys to wave at them."

I saw huge waterfalls and beautiful rivers and I looked out the window for so long I developed a pain in my neck. There was no chiropractor on the train.

Except for those short corridors between major cities, they will do away with passenger trains in this country one day, I predict, and you've got to wonder why the government is running a railroad in the first place. Especially our government.

That was one of the reasons I did this. To sit by a train window and watch two lovely states go by is a marvelous thing more people should do before it's too late.

And if you can't book a room with a shower, you can get a wet rag and some soap. On a train, you actually can get more washed that way.

July 1993

Delta's Ready When You Are, Toledo-Guy

I don't care what they do to the Georgia state flag. They can put a big peach on the thing as far as I'm concerned. They can put Deion Sanders's smiling face on it.

And let it be known that the opponents of the flag, with its reminiscence of the Confederate banner, will bring down that flag.

One way or the other, color it red, white, blue and gone. It's politically incorrect and all the things that are deemed such have no future in this country.

We elected Hillary Rodham Clinton and the ban on the gays in the military will be lifted. It's a done deal. Like it or not, the Georgia state flag has no chance either.

The issue on my mind is white Southerners like myself.

They don't like us. They don't trust us. They want to tell us why we're wrong. They want to tell us how we should change.

They is practically every s.o.b who isn't one of us.

I read a piece on the op-ed page of the *Constitution* written by somebody who in the jargon of my past "ain't from around here."

He wrote white Southerners are always looking back and that we should look forward. He said that about me.

I'm looking back? I live in one of the most progressive cities in the world. We built a subway to make Yankees feel at home. And I live in a region the rest of the country can't wait to move to.

A friend, also a native Southerner who shares my anger about the constant belittling of our kind and our place in this world, put it this way: "Nobody is going into an Atlanta bar tonight celebrating because they've just been transferred to New Jersey."

Damn straight.

I was having lunch at an Atlanta golf club recently. I was talking with friends.

A man sitting at another table heard me speaking and asked, "Where are you all from?" He was mocking me. He was mocking my Southern accent. He was sitting in Atlanta, Georgia, and was making fun of the way I speak.

He was from Toledo. He had been transferred to Atlanta. If I hadn't have been forty-six years old, skinny and a basic coward with a bad heart, I'd have punched him. I did, however, give him a severe verbal dressing-down.

I was in my doctor's office in Atlanta. One of the women who works there, a transplanted Northerner, asked how I pronounced the word *siren*. I said I pronounced it "si-reen." I was half kidding, but that is the way I heard the word pronounced when I was a child.

The woman laughed and said, "You Southerners really crack me up. You have a language all your own."

Yeah, we do. If you don't like it, go back home and stick your head in a snow bank.

They want to tell us how to speak, how to live, what to eat, what to think and they also want to tell us how they used to do it back in Buffalo.

Buffalo? What was the score? A hundred and ten to Zip.

The man writing on the op-ed page was writing about that bumper sticker that shows the old Confederate soldier and he's saying, "FERGIT HELL!" I don't go around sulking about the fact the South lost the Civil War. But I am aware that once upon a long time ago, a group of Americans saw fit to rebel against what they thought was an overbearing federal government. There is no record anywhere that indicates anybody in my family living in 1861 owned slaves. As a matter of fact, I come from a long line of sharecroppers, horse thieves and used-car dealers. But a few of them fought anyway — not to keep their slaves, because they didn't have any. I guess they simply thought it was the right thing to do at the time.

Whatever the reason, there was a citizenry that once saw fit to fight and die and I come from all that, and I look at those people as brave and gallant, and a frightful force until their hearts and their lands were burnt away.

I will never turn my back on that heritage.

But know this: I'm a white man and I'm a Southerner. And I'm sick of being told what is wrong with me from outside critics, and I'm tired of being stereotyped as a refugee from *God's Little Acre*.

If I've said it once, I've said it a thousand times, and I'll probably have to say it a thousand times again: Delta may be hurting financially, but it's still ready to take you back to Toledo whenever you're ready to go.

June 1993

Turnabout's Fair Play

A male friend showed me a grouping of photographs of women in a recent issue of *USA Today*. Women are coming after us, he said. "These are photographs of all the women running for the Senate."

There was a pack of them, to be sure. But read my words: I have nothing against women running for the Senate or being elected to the Senate. I'd even take Murphy Brown over Ted Kennedy.

I also have nothing against gains women have made in the business world, nor the fact they are achieving equal pay status with men in the workplace.

But let us look into the future here. We could have a woman president, an all-woman Congress, and women could take complete charge of the business world, but there would remain one ultimate inequity between men and women.

They have the babies, we don't.

They're the ones who have to go through morning sickness, carry around all that extra weight for nine months and endure the pain of childbirth, while all their husbands (providing they have husbands in this day and time) have to do is pace around in the waiting room.

I'm not saying all women are resentful of this inequity, but perhaps the most radical and militant portion of the women's movement is.

I don't think these women will ever rest and consider the sexes equal until men, too, have to start having babies.

This could never happen, you say? Did you read the other day the report that through genetic engineering it might be possible for people to live four hundred years? If scientists and researchers can figure out a way to add 325 years to the average life span, you don't think they'll eventually figure out a way for men to have babies? Certainly they will, and I think they should begin working immediately on such a project. It would solve a lot of modern-day problems.

"Honey," a wife could say, "I've really got a big project going on down at the firm. Why don't you have our next baby?" "But, sweetheart," the husband might reply, "I've got the member-guest golf tournament coming up at the club. If I were pregnant the extra weight would really louse up my swing."

"Darling, I had our last baby. It's your turn. That's only fair."

Fair. That's the key word here. How can men and women ever be completely equal and how can the reproduction process be totally fair until both sexes are able to give birth? I'm no scientist, so I don't have all the details worked out here, and there would be certain anatomical matters to be considered.

But we've sent a man to the moon, haven't we? And we're soon going to be able to live four hundred years.

Figuring a way for men, too, to have babies might be nothing compared with all the other things we've accomplished. Would I have a baby if science ever comes up with a way to make that possible? Sure I would. Equal is equal. And fair is fair, and I'd like to see an end to the war between the sexes.

But I'd wait a while, I think. Like at least until I was 225. I just don't think it's a good idea for kids, male or female, to have babies.

And that would also give me 180 years to find a wife (I'm old-fashioned) with whom I can get along.

Even for me, that should be plenty of time.

September 1992

A *Passion* For *Fashion*

Sadly, I've never been able to find a comfortable spot on the cutting edge of fashion although, Lord knows, I've tried.

When polyester leisure suits became the rage, I thought, "In order to find a comfortable spot on the cutting edge of fashion, I really need to get myself one of those polyester leisure suits."

But I kept waiting for the price to go down or a fast-food chain to offer one with a burger, so by the time I finally bought one — at a reduced price at a men's clothing outlet-store/sewer repair service — they already had been declared fire and health hazards and representatives from the Environmental Protection Agency showed up at my house and took mine away.

It was of a color seen only in emergency flare guns, if you must know.

Well, here I am with a similar decision to make. The latest thing in men's fashions, I have been noticing, is to wear a long-sleeved shirt with the top button buttoned with no tie.

A number of male television stars are into this look. I noticed comedian Gary Shandling dressed that way on television the other night.

I happened to pick up a copy of *Esquire* magazine in an airport and there were men in there in the same garb.

Most of these shirts, to me, at least, appear to be the sort your Uncle Carl used to wear. Uncle Carl was an aluminum siding salesman who used to visit once a year, pull on your ears and offer you guidance and encouragement with such advice as "Make yourself useful, kid, and go get me another beer."

Uncle Carl bought these shirts at a men's clothing outlet store/discount bowling alley. They were sort of shiny, had large collars and a vest pocket where Uncle Carl kept his package of Lucky Strikes.

(The late Uncle Carl, incidentally, died recently when shot

by an EPA agent while trying to light up a Lucky in a non-smoking area at a bowling alley.) "That's a really ugly shirt Uncle Carl is wearing," you used to think to yourself, but how did you know that in the '90s television stars would be wearing that same sort of shirt buttoned to the top? Nerds in high school used to wear those shirts, too, and I seem to recall they buttoned their top buttons. We used to laugh at them and the more violent among us used to take away their chemistry book and beat them over their heads with it.

"That's for wearing that shirt," nerds were told.

But look at me. I'm this far from going out and buying myself an Uncle Carl/nerd shirt, buttoning the top button and seeing if I can find a good, used Bunsen burner.

What may keep me from doing that, however, is I've also noticed just how often the cutting edge of fashion changes.

We've gone from leisure suits to Nehru jackets (although I'm not certain I have that in the right order), to shirts unbuttoned to the navel with gold chains dangling down to same, and now to the buttoned-up look.

The minute I go out and buy one of these shirts (or order it from a dead aluminum-siding salesman's clothing catalog), the fashion likely would change again and there I'll be looking like a pair of $3.50 Keds in Michael Jordan's shoe closet.

Since I didn't get in on this at the very beginning, the wise move might be for me to wait for the next fashion wind to blow and go with that.

Maybe bell-bottoms will come back. I have a pair Uncle Carl wore in the Navy. I can always dye them flare gun mauve.

June 1993

Johnny, You Done Us Proud

My mother was almost a complete invalid the last ten years of her life. She was confined to a hospital bed my stepfather had bought and placed in the living room so Mama could have some interaction with others.

Her eyesight had gone, and she wasn't able to read. I took her my books, but relatives had to read them to her.

Mama barely could see the living-room television, but one of her few pleasures was listening to it.

She was the primary individual in this world I wanted to impress.

That started early.

More than anything else, my mother wanted me to succeed.

She had been a victim of the Depression and had known what it is to do without. A thousand times she said to me, "I want you to have it better than I did."

Mama didn't know very much about newspapers, but when I announced I wanted to work for one, she didn't try to steer me somewhere else.

I got some breaks early in my career. I wound up editing a sports section in a major league town at twenty-three. Six years out of high school, I had fulfilled my lifetime's ambition.

Mama was delighted when I told her I had ascended to that lofty perch, but I'm not certain she actually understood what it was I was doing.

And then she knew I eventually turned to writing and had a column and produced a few books.

She seemed genuinely pleased with that. But, again, by then she wasn't able to read herself, and I'm not sure she was as proud of the fact I could write something a few people wanted to read as I was.

But then came Carson. When I told my mother I was going to fly all the way to California and sit next to Johnny Carson on "The Tonight Show," she was agog.

"Shut your mouth, son," she said.

"Shut your mouth" is Southern for, "You gotta be kidding."

Lewis with Johnny Carson on "The Tonight Show," 1985.

I was nervous on the show, not because I knew half the country would be watching me, but because I wanted to shine for Mama. I had the same feeling the first time she came to watch me play baseball.

I believe Mama went to her grave knowing I had, in fact, had it better than she did. I believe making it to "The Tonight Show" said to her all the sacrifices she made for me paid off and I hadn't blown it and wound up a seller of limited partnerships.

Carson was the Big Top for three decades. And the thing he should be honored for most is he made a lot of people's careers, but he broke no one's.

It was his show, to be sure, but he allowed his guests to steal their own moments. Letterman hogs it all. Carson shared, not just with the greats, but with the little people like newspaper columnists from Moreland, Georgia, as well.

I was on "The Tonight Show" twice. He was kind. He laughed at my stuff.

That he has retired now still hasn't sunk in completely. I felt that way when Sandy Koufax quit pitching and Arnold Palmer stopped winning golf tournaments.

But I was in Carson's Big Top twice and that made my poor, sick mother proud.

God bless you, Johnny Carson.

June 1992

CHAPTER

Eleven

"He was truly a great storyteller. And if there is a daily newspaper in heaven, I know what ol' Lewis is doing already."

J. DON JONES
MARIETTA, GEORGIA

Country Wasn't Always Cool

Las Vegas — Frank Sinatra is over at the Desert Inn. It's his seventy-seventh birthday, but who's really paying attention this week? Country music has taken over Las Vegas.

This town once belonged to Sinatra. To Sammy Davis, Jr. To Dean Martin. To Hollywood.

But look what's happening this week. Conway Twitty and George Jones have just left Bally's and Randy Travis has taken their place.

Others who've either just closed or who are just opening are Reba McIntyre, Lorrie Morgan, Doug Kershaw, Charlie Daniels and Dolly Parton.

It's Nashville West. Vegas entertainment is in boots and jeans and out of tuxedos.

One reason is, it's also National Rodeo Finals Week over at the coliseum where the University of Nevada-Las Vegas plays its basketball games.

Want to see the glitter of Vegas? It's still here, but what else you can see this week is the top rodeo cowboys riding and roping for money and national championships.

There's also something called the Miss Rodeo American Horsemanship competition.

I'm not sure what that is, but how can the rodeo folks get away with having a Miss Rodeo American HorseMANship competition? Alert the speech police.

There's also going to be Downtown Hoedown, a bucking horse and bull sale and a cowboy bowling tournament.

Nothing like a 7-10 split to chap your chaps.

But the primary reason country plays so well here, and everywhere else, is that it is no longer a stepchild of American music.

Country is now the No. 1-selling music in this country and it isn't just crossover stars like Garth Brooks who have done it.

Conway Twitty, who can plead to get a lost love back with the best of them, has been here, and George (Possum) Jones, whose voice even sounds like a steel guitar, was with him.

And Randy Travis. He brought back the traditional sound of country music when it was headed Lord-knows-where with too many rock-sounding licks and not enough twin-fiddle intros.

I'm playing a rather minor role in all this. Randy Travis is giving me a half hour to tell jokes at Bally's before he brings them to their feet with "On the Other Hand."

A couple of my boyhood friends, Danny Thompson and Dudley Stamps, were here with me for a couple of days and it was Dudley who surveyed this scene and asked "What was that song about being country a long time ago?"

"'I Was Country When Country Wasn't Cool,' by Barbara Mandrell," I, quite the country-music expert, answered.

"You know something?" Dudley went on. "That's us. We were country when they would laugh at you for listening to it."

We were. I gave up on rock'n'roll when the Beatles arrived, adopted country and have never looked back.

"Steve Smith had the best country jukebox I've ever heard," Dudley added.

Steve Smith's truck stop in Moreland was our gathering place as boys. You could get a great cheeseburger for a quarter, and I can still hear that jukebox filling the night with Ernest Tubb and Faron Young and Patsy Cline as we sat on the hoods of our cars in Steve's parking lot dreaming our dreams.

"I never thought back then," said Danny, "that three of us would be in Las Vegas one day with all these country acts and you being on stage telling jokes."

Neither did I. But country music and three ol' boys from Moreland, Georgia, have come a long ways. Keep us humble and grateful.

December 1992

Hissing For A Raise

I went in to see the big boss about a raise.

I was strip-searched twice and had to bow at the bronze sculpture of the big boss that sits outside his chambers.

Finally, I was ushered in.

There sat the big boss in a silk smoking jacket. The wood nymphs, who bore some resemblance to Milli and Vanilli, were on either side of him at his desk.

One fanned him with a palm. The other continued to whisper into his ear, "You're a swell guy."

"Sir," I began, "I have come to see you about a raise. I think it's ridiculous what you're paying me when guys with lifetime batting averages of .240 are making $6 million a year."

A puzzled look came across the big boss's face.

"What in hell are you talking about?" he asked puzzledly.

"I'm talking about the fact that baseball players who couldn't hit a curveball if they had two weeks' notice it was coming are making obscene amounts of money and I'm being paid a pittance in comparison."

The big boss's face turned red. The two wood nymphs glared at me.

"You're asking me for a raise based on what ballplayers are making?" the big boss roared across the desk.

"I'm not running a baseball team here," he roared on, "I'm running a newspaper."

I held my ground.

"I'm aware of that, sir," I said. "But my point is that I believe that if you counted my good columns against my bad ones the way batting averages are compiled, I'd be way ahead of .240 — especially if you discount the columns I wrote with a hangover, the ones I wrote when I was deathly ill in Acapulco, and the ones I wrote at home while the bug guy was spraying.

"I think my average would be considerably above .300, which would win you a batting title and get you a multiyear deal worth the defense budget and lots of women."

The big boss listened to my argument and I sensed he felt my points were ringed with some degree of truth. I sensed all that because he had stopped rubbing the right thigh of the wood nymph waving the palm.

"I'll tell you what I'm going to do," the big boss began. "I'm going to give you a raise because I admire your spunk.

"But it won't be one like some jerk ballplayer gets for occasionally getting his uniform dirty.

"If I ran this company like a ball team, I'd be like a homeless snake — I wouldn't have a pit to hiss in. Now get out of here and go back to work."

As I bowed to the sculpture again on my way out, I thought, "If the big boss did run this company like a ball team, I wonder what I would have gotten?" Probably millions, part ownership in the company and a wood nymph to be named later.

December 1990

Stripe Of A Different Snake

There are two schools of thought regarding snakes.

One is the school that always points out snakes aren't really the epitome of evil and most of them aren't poisonous anyway, so don't be afraid of them.

The other school says don't talk to me about no snakes.

I'm a member of the second group.

I'm afraid of snakes. No, I'm terrified at even the thought of a snake. I don't even like to look at pictures of snakes.

When I was a kid, some idiot was always bringing a snake to school to frighten girls. I tried to hide my fear of snakes back then so I wouldn't be called a sissy.

Being called a sissy was a hard fate. It meant you threw a baseball with too much wrist, were overprotected by your mother and walked funny.

I was able to remain in the snake closet until one day the school bully, Frankie Garfield, brought a snake to school and said to me, "Hold my snake while I go beat up a couple of fourth-graders."

What a dilemma. I had rather put my hand in a lawnmower blade than touch a snake. But if I didn't do what Frankie told me to do, he would do the fist dance on my face.

I opted for the fist dance. Frankie let me have one upside the head and called me a sissy, but I didn't have to touch the snake.

The reason I bring all this up is, I was thumbing through the paper the other day and there was an article in the Home and Garden section about garter snakes.

It was an article that people who aren't afraid of snakes always write. It said garter snakes can live in urban and suburban surroundings, but it's silly to be afraid of them or attempt to kill them because they aren't poisonous and they're important to the ecological balance.

"It's shameless to destroy these snakes," the article said.

It also quoted an Atlanta naturalist as saying snakes in this country with longitudinal stripes, like the garter snake, aren't poisonous.

I don't care. In the first place, I'm not hanging around a snake long enough, or getting close enough, to see if it has longitudinal stripes or not.

In the second place, I'm not absolutely certain about the difference between longitudinal stripes and latitudinal stripes. It's always one of those things I've had trouble remembering, like which number to invert when dividing fractions.

I've written often about my theory that if you figure there's really only one kind of snake and it will bite you given half a chance, then you won't ever make a mistake and misread a snake's stripes and wind up having to slice yourself with a pocketknife to suck out the poison.

Blech!

To me, there is only one kind of snake, the dreaded copperheaded water rattler. If you run from it, it will chase you. If you lock yourself inside your house and hide in a closet, it will wait outside until you finally come out because copperheaded water rattlers have X-ray vision and can see you in there.

And even if you stay in the closet for, say, a week, and the snake has to leave, the copperheaded water rattler knows where you work.

To anybody who wants to tell me otherwise, save your breath. It's my phobia and I'm sticking to it.

June 1992

Trashing TV By Remote Control

The television remote control device is one of the few things mechanical or electronic I can successfully operate.

By that I mean I can turn the television on, I can turn it off, I can control the volume and I can switch the channels.

It is also one of the few modern conveniences I consider a true convenience.

The electric toothbrush certainly isn't. Somebody gave me one of those. I put the toothpaste on the brush, but when I hit the juice, the brush vibrates so violently by the time I get it to my mouth, it has shaken the toothpaste off. Toothpaste in your eyes burns.

The automatic coffee maker really isn't automatic. If it were automatic it would locate those little packs of coffee I can never find in my kitchen and then pour the water in itself.

But the remote control, a.k.a. the "magic clicker." Do you realize what we had to do before we had those? We actually had to get up off our rears, walk over to the set and manually turn the channel changer.

Had it not been for the magic clicker, I wouldn't have had the warm, wonderful experience I had recently.

I had retired early. I turned on the television in my bedroom.

"I'll lie here," I said to myself, "and watch a good movie."

I knew I could use the magic clicker to find one. I wouldn't have to jump up and out of bed switching channels in my search.

I began at the lower end of the channel range where HBO and Cinemax and the Movie Channel are located.

On one, fourteen people were shooting automatic weapons at one another. Blood was gushing. I hit the magic clicker.

On the next channel a man and a

woman were engaged in heated dialogue. In thirty seconds they each used the "f" word in a veritable buffet of variations. There was a time you couldn't say "pregnant" on television.

On to the third channel. Jim and Margaret Anderson didn't even sleep together on "Father Knows Best." There was enough skin showing in the first thirty seconds of the movie showing on this particular channel to reupholster an entire Greyhound bus.

So on I went. Through the mindless sitcoms of the network channels.

Through CNN and war and famine and disease and Hillary. Through TNN and men in cowboy hats and women in dire need of Nordic Trackers line-dancing.

And then to TNT. They were showing "Lassie" movies on TNT. Can you imagine that? In the quagmire of sex and violence, midst the medium that spawned "Beavis and Butt-head" and rock videos and the ever-increasing innuendos of the sitcoms, I found Lassie.

What I watched, in its entirety, was *Son of Lassie*, colorized, but otherwise as pure as ever.

Peter Lawford, of all people, was an RAF pilot and he was shot down behind Nazi lines with Laddie, Lassie's own.

They become separated and Laddie goes on the inevitable search to find his master. There were fresh-faced, laughing children in the movie and good people fighting evil and one determined dog.

It was my best television moment since Aunt Bea went to Mount Pilot and Andy and Opie made her feel unneeded by keeping the house spotless while she was away.

Nobody used the "f" word. Nobody blew off anybody else's head. Nobody got naked.

It's still in that box, though limited. Entertainment without the raunch. You just have to look for it, and the magic clicker, bless it, puts it at your fingertips.

See Laddie run. I dreamt that night the Beav and I went spitting off a bridge.

October 1993

Ginsu Loses The Point

One doesn't know how much one values one's I-told-you-so finger until somebody wants to cut off one's I-told-you-so finger.

I am speaking here, in my case, of my right pointer finger; the one I shake in your face and say, "Didn't I tell you Ross Perot would kick Al Gore's fanny in the NAFTA debate?" (I don't know one thing about NAFTA, except that if Bill Clinton is for it, I'm against it. It's called the politics of the happily uninformed.) Since back in the spring certain known practitioners of medicine have been wanting to cut off that finger at the first joint.

That is because during my heart valve surgery at that time, a blood clot formed on the tip of that finger and caused it to turn completely black.

"We need to take the tip of that finger off," said doctors at Emory Hospital.

The theory was that portion of my finger was dead and gone. It would never recover, never return to its previous self.

I must admit I've had my own doubts. The black portion of the tip was a hardened crust.

"That will come off," said doctors, "and there will be bone exposed and you'll lose the use of the finger."

Still, I refused to have the tip of the finger amputated. I recently visited Virginia, incidentally, where Lorena Bobbitt is still loose, so I kept my right hand in my pocket.

As long as that hard, black outer crust was attached to my finger, I was able to get by fairly nicely.

When I pointed it at somebody and said, "I told you we'd get bogged down in a no-win situation in Somalia," the fact the end of it looked like it had been run over in the train wreck scene of *The Fugitive* made it even more imposing.

There were a few things I had to change. Because the nail has been sensitive, I've had to learn to type with one less finger.

And to compensate, I had to shelve my '50s-vintage manual typewriter for an electric, whose keys offer less resistance. But

I am still yet to touch a computer, which I consider to be the work of the devil.

There were other changes I had to make, but they are of a more personal nature, and despite the fact a woman cutting off a man's skaddodah (Mongolian term) is now front page news, I still think it best to spare you details.

The finger's condition did not keep me from playing golf, my passion, however. That particular finger, thankfully, plays very little part in the golf grip or swing.

But, this. I was playing the par five, seventh hole at the beautiful Ansley Golf Club last week. I swung a six-iron. The blackened, hard-crusted tip of my finger fell off.

Fell off.

What was underneath it was what appeared to be a rather nasty-looking combination of caked-blood and pinkish, ultra-sensitive tissue.

But it didn't hurt. I continued the hole, as a matter of fact, and, for the record, I parred it. Let the tip of Nick Faldo's finger fall off after hitting a six-iron and see if he still pars the hole.

"What did you do with the part of the finger that fell off?" I naturally was asked when recounting the story.

Simple. Picked it up off the fairway, put it in my pocket and used it to mark my ball when I reached the green.

I think that finger is going to make it. It has looked better each day. And to those who insisted upon taking it from me, it points now.

Ginsu skaddodah. That's Mongolian for either, "Get away from me with that knife," or, "I told you so."

November 1993

CHAPTER

Twelve

"I can't find a babysitter so I am staying home from work on this day of his funeral, feeling much like a relative who couldn't muster the plane fare needed to fly home. I only hope he knew during his life how much he enriched our understanding and perspective of our own lives."

BARBARA WATTERS
ROSWELL, GEORGIA

To Lewis Grizzard
With best wishes,

Nancy Reagan

I *Caught* One THIS *Long*

Quadra Island, British Columbia — The most exciting places to go are the places where, when you get there, you have to look on a map to see where you are.

So when I finally arrived here, I scrounged a world atlas and found myself. I was off Vancouver Island, which is across the Strait of Georgia off the coast of Canada's western province, British Columbia.

What I came to do was fish for salmon with former professional football player Dick Butkus and have it taped for the ESPN television program "Suzuki's Great Outdoors." Dick Butkus is the host.

Getting here was something. I left from Orlando. I flew to Salt Lake City, to Portland and then to Vancouver.

In Vancouver, I waited in line for an hour with half the Asian peoples on Earth to get through customs. Then I climbed aboard an orange crate and flew to Campbell River, British Columbia, which is on Vancouver Island.

After that I took a van and a ferry and I arrived at the April Point Fishing Lodge 16 1/2 hours later.

The only kind of fish I had ever caught before were catfish, crappie and bream. My grandfather used to take me fishing in local ponds when I was a boy.

But I gave up fishing. I didn't like handling the bait. I didn't like handling the fish, and I didn't want to eat anything that would eat anything as nasty as fish bait.

So I'm not certain how I got talked into this. I didn't even get paid. But after sitting around for three months trying to get over heart surgery, I was ready to do something besides watching the coffee couple play suckface on television, and complaining about my chest feeling like I had recently dived atop an exploding grenade.

The first thing I had to do was to learn to pronounce the word "salmon." The closest I'd ever been to one before was when my mother used to fry salmon patties that came from a

Lewis reeling in the crappie during a 1972 outing.

can. We pronounced it SAL-mon, as in Sal Mineo, because it has an "L" in it.

But here I was told the "L" was silent, and it was SAA-mon. I tried my best to say it that way.

So we went out one chilly morning into the choppy Strait of Georgia. We were in a very small boat, I thought. In this small boat was Dick Butkus, a very large man, not to mention myself, a cameraperson, a soundperson, and the fishing guide, also a person.

It was my kind of fishing. The guide cut the head off the herring, which is what salmon eat, and put the rest of it on my hook. He dropped the hook into the water and we trolled.

I got five coho salmon to the boat, which, miraculously, never turned over. The guide took each fish off the hook, showed it to the cameraperson and then tossed it back into the water.

I never touched a single piece of bait. I never touched a fish. I ate prime rib back at the lodge.

I actually would have caught more salmon (my largest was about seven pounds, said the guide) if I hadn't been doing a fishing show and the director hadn't said to me at least a couple of times, "Stop reeling in until we can get the sun on your face."

Besides being a large man, Dick Butkus is a very nice man. He caught only one coho salmon, but he didn't pick me up and throw me into the Strait of Georgia because it was his show and I still caught five times the fish he did.

I left Quadra Island on a floatplane back to Vancouver. I felt completely safe. I figured anything goes wrong here, we can just land right on the water two thousand feet directly below us.

Look for me this fall fishing with Dick Butkus on "Suzuki's Great Outdoors." If you have any trouble distinguishing between me and ol' No. 51 of the Chicago Bears, I'm the one catching all the saamon.

July 1993

Confessions Of An Ex-Athlete

The phone rings. "Is this Mr. Grizzard?"

"Yes."

"Mr. Lewis Grizzard?"

"Speaking."

"Mr. Grizzard, this is the *Newnan Times-Herald* in Newnan, Georgia."

"What a pleasant surprise. My hometown newspaper's calling."

"Mr. Grizzard, we have some questions for you."

"Is this about erecting a statue of me on the courthouse square?"

"No, Mr. Grizzard. What we want to know is, did you or did you not play basketball and baseball on the varsity Newnan High teams from 1962 through 1964?"

"I did."

"Mr. Grizzard, are you aware of the trend of ex-athletes turning in their schools for various violations?"

"You mean like Eric Ramsey of Auburn and Gene Jelks of the University of Alabama?"

"Precisely."

"Well, I've read a little here and there. Both Ramsey and Jelks have told the press they received illegal payments from coaches and alumni while they were at school."

"That is correct."

"What does that have to do with me?"

"The *Times-Herald* has reason to believe that while you were an athlete at Newnan High you might have received illegal offerings from coaches and alumni."

"You're not talking about the food they used to buy us on road trips, are you?"

"So, you admit it."

"Well, I guess so. We played a basketball game one night against Headland High School in suburban Atlanta and after the game the bus stopped at Shoney's and we all got a free dinner."

"And what did you have, Mr. Grizzard?"

"Well, it's been thirty years but I seem to recall something about ordering the Half Pound o' Ground Round, medium well."

"And how about strawberry pie for dessert?"

"I might have had that, but I'm not sure."

"Don't dally around with us, Mr. Grizzard. Several former teammates have told us the starting team — of which you were a member — all had strawberry pie for dessert, which is a violation of the Georgia High School Scholastic Association rules of no dessert with road game meals."

"OK, I had the pie, but I didn't inhale."

"Is it also true, Mr. Grizzard, that on the way home from a road trip baseball game the coach bought you two sliced pork barbecue sandwiches at Sprayberry's Barbecue in Newnan?"

"That's true, but I paid for my own onion rings."

"Are you sure?"

"Yeah, the coach ran out of money."

"Might a school booster have paid for your onion rings?"

"We didn't have any school boosters."

"Why is that?"

"We were 1-12 at the time."

"Mr. Grizzard, are you certain you aren't trying to cover up anything? Many former athletes are coming clean about how they were taken advantage of during their school days."

"Well, the coaching staff didn't awaken me every morning to make certain I was in class on time, and they didn't come home with me at night to make certain I did my homework, and they gave me all that free food, so I guess you could say they used me for my athletic prowess and nothing else."

"May we quote you on that, Mr. Grizzard?"

"As long as you don't point out that when we got jock itch they gave us free powder. I'd hate to get my alma mater in any trouble."

"How quaint. See you on the front page."

November 1992

Duffs In The Buff

I am not at liberty to divulge the name or location of the golf course where the incident I soon will describe took place.

The reason for that is that the developer and owner of the course told me not to, and he is a very large man who seems to be the sort of person one would be wise not to cross.

Allow me to say, however, this man can also be trusted at his word, and there are other witnesses to the incident, so I believe it to be true without a shade of doubt.

The owner of the course was in his office one afternoon recently and the young woman who drives his beverage cart came running in, out of breath, and visibly stunned.

The more she tried to talk, the more she was unable to get the words out.

"Slow down," said the owner. "Take a deep breath and then tell me what on Earth the trouble is."

The young woman finally regained her composure and said, "There are four men out on thirteen playing naked."

I play a lot of golf and I know a lot of weird stories.

I also know of the infamous Ft. Worth Rule most other male golfers know, but it cannot be repeated here.

But I had never heard of anybody playing golf naked.

"This was in broad daylight?" I asked the owner of the course as he began to relate the story.

"Broad daylight," he said.

I asked him to continue.

"I got into a cart and rode down to see for myself," he went on. "Sure enough, there were four of them, butt naked, except for their shoes and socks.

"They didn't see me coming at first. I drove around and picked up all their clothes. When they finally saw me, I said, 'What's going on here, boys?'

"I could tell they were pretty drunk. One tried to explain they'd bet if one didn't get across the water, he'd have to play the hole naked, and one thing led to another.

There were few things in life Lewis enjoyed as much as golf.

"They apologized and asked for their clothes. I said, 'Y'all seem to be enjoying yourselves so much, just keep going.' I made them tee off and play the next hole naked, too. They were embarrassed as hell. One of them even started crying."

"So, did you finally give them their clothes back?" I asked.

"Yeah, and they said, 'Well, I guess we can't come back here any more?'

"I said, 'Not for a while, boys. We'll need some time to get over this.'"

I mentioned I've heard a lot of golf stories. There was one in a recent national golf magazine issue about a guy, angry over being far behind his opponent in a match, urinating on his opponent's ball.

The magazine consulted a rules expert who said if an opponent urinated on your golf ball, it would clearly be inside the rules to "lift, clean and place your ball."

Said the magazine to the rules expert, "*You* lift, clean and place the ball."

I've also heard of golf shots hitting and killing birds in flight; one golfer going home and getting his gun and coming back to the course and shooting his opponent over an argument regarding whether or not a putt should have been conceded; and I saw a man shank a ball so badly against a strong wind in Scotland, it wound up twenty yards behind him.

But naked golfing is a new one. I've been searching for a moral to this story, but one doesn't readily unveil itself. I do, however, realize golf is supposedly a gentlemen's game and gentlemen normally don't get naked in public.

On the other hand, a bet's a bet.

So there's a dilemma here. I'd simply say, watch what you wager, not to mention what you waggle.

June 1992

Of Armed Schools And Task Forces

I can't imagine children shooting and killing other children in school. Can't figure out how it can happen. Can't deal with it really. I come from another time. I graduated from Newnan High School in 1964.

If they caught you chewing gum they took you outside and flogged you.

Well, they didn't do that, but they made you write "I am a juicy fruit" fourteen thousand times on the chalk board.

Shoot somebody? Mrs. Evans, the librarian, made the boys take off their watches and the girls take off their bracelets so they wouldn't scratch the tables when they sat down to read.

When students walked in the halls, boys and girls couldn't be closer than five feet to each other. Teachers carried rulers around with them.

O.P. Evans, the principal, read biblical warnings against disrespecting authority at assembly meetings. He would cite a school rule and bellow in his frightful voice, "Just challenge us! Just challenge us!" Shoot somebody? I was afraid to breathe.

I also got a great education and never feared for my life.

One kid blows another kid away at Atlanta's Harper High School. The dead kid is fifteen. In 1989 another fifteen-year-old was beaten to death at Harper High.

You know what one of the problems is? Get some of the reaction to the Tuesday shooting.

The mother of the suspected murderer said her son's "tragic side of the story hasn't been told."

There we go again. The criminal as victim. He's still alive, isn't he? Vanessa Shareef, described as The Atlanta Project's Harper Cluster coordinator, had this to say: "From what I get talking to my child and others, the boy (who did the shooting) didn't feel he had an option of anyone to talk to, anyone who was listening, anyone who would address the fact that he was getting beaten by these other boys. The children at the school, they feel there was some justification (for the shooting), I'm sad to say."

Poor misunderstood kid. He's getting pushed around and nobody will listen to him, so he shoots a fellow classmate in the back.

And some fellow students think he was justified.

My God.

But not to worry. We've got a task force on the situation now. Has there ever been a task force in the history of task forces that accomplished anything? Here's what an article in the paper said: "A new state task force on violence in schools kicked off Wednesday with a brainstorming session on how to develop safe schools without creating armed camps of shakedowns and metal detectors."

". . . without creating armed camps?" I've got news for the state task force. Some of our schools already are armed camps. The problem is it's the kids who are armed.

If it takes armed camps of shakedowns and metal detectors to stop the violence, then why the hell not? I wouldn't care if they strip-searched my kid three times before lunch if it lessened the chances of him or her getting shot by fifth period.

"The task force will hold public hearings throughout the state this month and compile a preliminary report," said the papers.

Public hearings and preliminary reports. Horse manure. Somebody, like parents and school officials, have to get mad and mean and dare the punks to challenge them. O. P. Evans would have called up the National Guard.

At one local high school where a policeman carries a gun in the hallway, a student said of the cop's presence: "It sucks."

Not nearly as much, young fellow, as being dead.

September 1993

Be Sweet

Whenever I left my late mother's home, and we are talking a period of over forty years, she would always end her goodbyes with these two words: "Be sweet."

When I was a child on my way to a friend's birthday party, I suppose that meant not to stick my finger in the cake or do a lot of whining and crying.

In my teen years it meant not to steal any hubcaps.

As an adult, I guess now she was beseeching me not to rob a liquor store, engage in any insider trading, and to go out amongst them each day with a smile and agreeable disposition.

I can't recall sticking my finger into too many birthday cakes, but I very likely ignored the part about no whining nor crying when things didn't go my way on occasion — such as when I pinned the tail on the donkey's esophagus.

I never stole a hubcap. Not one.

As an adult I've never robbed anything nor have I engaged in much of any kind of trading that was profitable.

But that other stuff — the daily smile, the agreeable disposition — well, I've had my failures.

I notoriously have not been sweet to such individuals as waiters and waitresses I've deemed slow or unable to service correctly what I considered to be the simplest of orders.

Many a rental car clerk has known my verbal wrath, not to mention motel housekeepers who bang on my door too quickly after the first crow of morning, people I don't know who address me as "buddy" and liberals.

Yet, my mother's words, so simple, were so implicit: Be sweet.

We have recognized the terror that is the violence amongst us today. Television has moved it out front of eating disorders, Satan worship, and women who run with wolves, which is a certain sign it is presently the No. 1 discussable public issue.

The drive-by shootings. Another kid shot dead in the school. The yellow police-line tape and pools of drying blood on a mean street on the eleven o'clock news.

The money we will spend, the hours we will study and discuss in an effort to find a solution.

But isn't it right there in Miss Christine's words — Be sweet? We aren't sweet. The truth is we don't honor sweet. We don't even like sweet. Sweet is weak. Women go to classes to learn not to be sweet.

Men. We've got an entire generation of young toughs out there who are drunk and dying on their own testosterone.

Being sweet can get you killed in that group.

It's a manhood thing. An Atlanta Falcons football player, Andre Rison, decides somebody has challenged his manhood outside an Atlanta nightclub. So he goes to his car and gets his gun.

There's this "dis" thing. It's street talk for "disrespect." I've got dis big gun here. Respect me or I'll shoot you.

No. No. Be sweet.

Be kind and be gentle. Be tolerant. Be forgiving and slow to anger.

Be tender and be able to cry. Be kind to old people and dogs and don't cut off any part of anybody else's anatomy.

Be loving. Be tender. Share. Don't pout. Don't be so loud. Hold a puppy. Kiss a hand. Put your arms around a frightened child.

Make an outstanding athletic play and then don't do The King Tut Butt Strut to bring attention to yourself and point to the inadequacies of the vanquished.

Be sweet. The wonders that might do. The wonders that just might do. I can still hear you, Mama.

January 1994

Surviving The Eating Season

Eating Season has begun. It starts on Thanksgiving Day and runs all the way through New Year's.

A lot of people dread the coming of Eating Season and all those dinner parties because they know they are going to gain weight.

I don't have that problem. I could eat a pickup truckload of food and still not gain weight.

The politically correct way to describe me is "gooless" or "lard-deficient."

The politically incorrect way to describe me is, "The man's a walking two-iron."

I'm not certain why I never gain weight no matter what I eat; somebody suggested I had a high metabolism.

I went to my doctor, but he couldn't find one.

Somebody else suggested I might have a tapeworm, but the X-rays were negative.

That long thing going from my neck to my stomach was an undigested vermicelli noodle left over from the spaghetti dinner I had the night before, which also included buttered French bread, and a pint of ice cream covered in chocolate sauce with whipped cream on top.

Many probably are saying, "All this pipe cleaner is trying to do is rub it in. I could simply be in the same room with a pint of ice cream and gain four pounds."

Not true.

Not only am I not trying to rub in the fact I can soar through Eating Season with no weight gain, I also have some advice for those who emerge each year from Eating Season having put on the weight of the left side of a Little League infield.

Because I've never had that problem, I have been keenly interested in those who do, having watched their behavior around food during the Eating Season, and hereby offer these tips on how not to come out of the holidays with the fear that if somebody tied you to a stake in the ground with a rope, you easily could be mistaken for the Sea World blimp:

Eat Standing Up at Holiday Parties — You've got your drink in one hand, which leaves only the other hand free to hold food, which means it's going to be difficult to pick up an entire smoked turkey. Sit down with a plate and both hands free, and the Sea World blimp couldn't get airborne with you in it.

Chew Thoroughly and Swallow Before Putting Any More Food in Your Mouth — This will cut down on the amount of time you have to eat. I realize a piece of coconut cake goes great mixed in your mouth with four melon balls and a leg of lamb, but you've got to work with me here.

Remember There Will Be Other Opportunities to Eat — Pigs don't know that. That's why pigs gorge. But you should know that, so get your head out of the sweet potato souffle.

Don't Ask for Leftovers to Take Home for Your Dog at Seasonal Gatherings — You don't even have a dog.

Don't Say to Yourself, "I'll Go on a Diet in January." — Don't kid yourself. I looked up "before" in the dictionary and your picture was next to it.

Don't Eat Anything Bigger Than Your Head — Sound advice, so put down that cheese ball.

Hoe handle here says, "Good luck."

December 1992

CHAPTER

Thirteen

"A 5.3-magnitude quake in Southern California the afternoon of March 20? Suspicions abound that this disturbance was merely Lewis and Catfish rumbling through the heavens on their way to Mama's for fried chicken and scratch biscuits."

ANNA WILLIAMS
LEESVILLE, SOUTH CAROLINA

ILLUSTRATION BY DAVID BOYD

Women In Running Shoes Brought To Heel

WASHINGTON — My ride was late, so as I waited on the sidewalk in downtown Washington, I people-watched.

I had seen the phenomenon I'm about to discuss in other large cities, but here in Washington there seemed to be even more instances of it.

I'm speaking of the fact that when females in the workplace are out of their offices, many are now walking around in their otherwise attractive outfits in running shoes.

I am told that women wear these shoes to lunch and to and from work, but once they are in their offices they put on regular shoes, ones with heels that are more suited to the rest of their clothing.

I asked a female colleague about this once and she explained, "We do it for comfort. You just can't imagine how doing a lot of walking in heels can absolutely kill your feet."

I can understand that. I've never personally done a lot of walking (or any walking for that matter) in a pair of heels, but I can imagine how one's feet would feel afterward.

Still, I've got to say this: Comfort or no comfort, wearing a pair of running shoes with a dress does to the attractiveness of a woman what a large tattoo does to a man. It's downright displeasing to the eye. In a word — ugly.

And I hate to use the "T" word, but I feel compelled.

It's Tacky.

At a gathering later in the evening, I asked a Washington woman, who had had the good sense not to show up at a cocktail party wearing a pair of Reeboks, why this practice seemed so prevalent in Washington.

"I don't think it has anything to do with politics," she said.

"Maybe Washington women just have to walk more than women in other cities. Why do you ask?" Diplomacy has never been my strong suit. I looked at her square in her eyes and said, "Because it's tacky."

She threw a sausage ball at me and then huffed away in disgust.

But that didn't change my opinion. I don't think I have any sort of foot fetish, but women in sexy shoes have always caught my eye.

I recall the first time I saw Kathy Sue Loudermilk in a pair of high heels. It was at the annual Moreland Fourth of July barbecue. She was also wearing her tight pink sweater (the one they retired in the trophy case when she graduated from high school), a pair of short shorts and eight-inch spike heels.

When the Baptist preacher, who was helping make the coleslaw, saw her, he said, "Lord, thy do make some lovely things."

I don't think he was talking about the onions he was putting in the coleslaw.

Said my boyhood friend and idol, Weyman C. Wannamaker, Jr., a great American, when he saw Kathy Sue, "You put something besides them heels on that body and you done put retreads on a Rolls Royce."

And here I stand on a downtown sidewalk in our nation's capital and eight out of ten women I see look like they went to the Sears tire store to shop for shoes.

The Lord does, indeed, make some lovely things, and I'm certain the almighty had no intention they walk around in what amounts to glorified, overpriced, rubber-soled clodhoppers.

Your feet hurt, ladies? See Dr. Scholl.

Tacky. Tacky. Tacky.

I think I have made myself abundantly clear.

December 1990

On The Road With The Author From Hell

Here's the way the story was reported in the Atlanta newspapers: "Not everyone thinks Georgia humorist and *Atlanta Journal-Constitution* columnist Lewis Grizzard is a hoot.

"Literary escorts — who cart visiting writers from interview to interview — vote annually on the Golden Dart Board Award, better known as the Author from Hell Award.

"The escorts voted Grizzard a lifetime award at a recent publishing industry convention in Miami. His offenses: insensitivity and refusal to leave for interviews when there's a playoff game on television. In Grizzard's absence, fellow humorist and Decatur native, Roy Blount, Jr., accepted the award, 'with apologies on behalf of the state of Georgia.'"

Well, stitch my britches, as they say at the *New Yorker* when Roy Blount, Jr. turns in another hilarious piece.

In the first place, if they had told me of the award and had invited me, I'd have come to Miami to accept it myself.

In the second place, if there are any apologies to be made here, I'll make them myself.

I apologize to the escort in Cleveland, who nearly ran head-on into a semi because she was so short she couldn't see over the steering wheel, for saying, "My God, lady, this is a book tour, not a performance by Joey Chitwood and the Hell Drivers." I didn't realize she had something in her good eye.

I do not apologize for not wanting to leave a Braves-Pirates playoff game to drive halfway across New Orleans to some campus radio station whose signal wouldn't reach to the gymnasium.

In the third place, allow me to explain a little further how this escort thing works: This isn't one of those deals where you look in a phone book and call Foxy Lady Escort Service for someone to accompany you to the Christian Science Reading Room, or wherever.

When an author has a book published, the publisher foots the bill for a publicity tour. The author goes from city to city doing radio, television and newspaper interviews about his or her book.

Because it's cheaper than limousines, the publisher hires a literary escort in each city — usually one who owns a very old and small car — to motor the author around the city.

The author is very tired because it's the thirteenth day of the tour and he or she has just flown in from St. Louis where the day's previous escort had brought along her cat and some air-head at a television station had asked, "So, tell us what your book is about."

There are more interviews like that scheduled this day unless the kid with a Mr. Microphone, who got on the list somehow, cancels. In that case, you can have lunch.

Don't get me wrong. I've had some very nice escorts over the past three hundred years I've been doing book tours. One in Jacksonville brought Tab, my favorite drink, with her. Do you know how hard it is to find Tab anymore? The lady in Dallas always takes me to my favorite barbecue place there, Sonny Bryan's (if there's time for lunch), and I fell in love with my escort in Nashville once. (Unfortunately, she was married to a successful picker.) And not all interviews are bad ones, either. I even had an interviewer in Chicago once who had read the book. Maybe that's why he gave me such a bad review.

Still, it's not my style going around being the author from hell, even during a publicity tour from the same locale. So I'll try to be better this fall. Besides, it doesn't look like the Braves are going to make the playoffs this year anyway.

And I just thought of another great escort I had in Birmingham. She brought along her husband to drive, and I said to her, "You're the best escort I've ever had."

And they call me insensitive.

June 1993

Wasting Time And Money

My watch disappeared the other day, quite mysteriously. I was in a hotel room, and I distinctly remember taking it off before I went into the shower.

But after the shower, a shave and getting dressed, I couldn't find my watch anywhere.

I looked everywhere for it. I looked under the bed. I looked under the cushions of the sofa. I looked in the pockets of the pants I had on before my shower.

But no watch. But no big deal, either.

I only paid $29.95 for it about a year ago at Bloomingdale's in New York. I simply said to myself, "I'll go buy another watch."

I went down to a shop in the lobby of the hotel and looked over its collection of watches, and in about nine seconds I picked out another one. I splurged a little. It cost $37.95.

I remain convinced that spending a lot of money on a watch is a ridiculous excess.

What do you want in a watch? You want it to give you the correct time, give or take a minute or so, don't you? That's really all you want out of a watch. But some people go out and spend thousands on a watch that is gold and has diamonds, and they look at theirs and it says sixteen minutes after four, the same as mine that cost me less than forty bucks.

But they lose theirs and it's panic time. I lose mine and for pocket change I've got another one.

I admit I did buy a fairly expensive watch once. I was in Lucerne and you know the great deals you can get on a watch in Switzerland.

I went into a place and spent $200 on a watch. A few months later, I was playing golf and it was very hot and some moisture got inside my $200 watch. A cloud formed inside of it, so I couldn't look down at it and tell the time anymore.

That's when I decided spending any sum over two figures was stupid when you go buy a watch.

So you've got a Rolex. I'm not impressed. Somebody walks up to the both of us and asks, "Have you got the time?" and I will be just as qualified as you to answer and you have spent what you can buy a car for on your watch, and I've spent peanuts.

Somebody might hit you in the head and steal your Rolex. Nobody would waste their time stealing mine.

I might buy an expensive watch if it had extras an inexpensive one doesn't.

If the thing told me not only the time, but also the weather forecast, West Coast baseball scores, my horoscope, how the market is doing, what club to hit, my cholesterol count, or whether or not I'm being lied to, that's one thing. But an expensive watch doesn't give you any more information than an inexpensive one.

So some watches also give you the day of the week and the day of the month.

If I get confused about either of these, all I have to do is plunk down a quarter for a newspaper and I've got that information, plus what Nelson Mandela said the day before.

Just think what would happen if all the people who buy expensive watches would buy cheap ones, and give what they save to the homeless. Or to the American Cancer Society. Or to the American Heart Association. Or to Donald Trump to help him get out of debt. Or to the Oakland A's to help them pay Jose Canseco's new $23 million contract.

We could solve a lot of problems with that money, and everybody would still know what time it is and how long they can hold their breath. According to my $37 watch, it's nine minutes after nine in the morning as I finish this column.

I think I'll take the rest of the day off.

September 1990

Pining Away In Texas

LUBBOCK, Texas — We got in the car and drove to Amarillo. It's maybe 120 miles from Lubbock. All of them are flat. The fellow driving was a native of these West Texas parts.

I wanted to know what happened to all the trees.

There weren't any. Just miles and miles of scenery with very little to see.

OK, I did see a few trees. One was growing in the midst of a multi-acre spread some Texan probably calls "my little farm."

I had met a Texas farmer earlier and he had said, "I don't have but seventeen thousand acres."

"I wonder how that one tree got in the middle of all that land?" I said to the guy driving.

"I don't know," he said. "But a lot of times I've seen a tree like that and a farmer was cutting it down so he didn't have to plow around it."

"There are so few trees, it seems like a crime to cut one down," I said.

"You don't plow much, do you?" asked my Texas companion.

We drove past Happy, Texas. There were cars with bumper stickers that read: "Happy, Texas — The town without a frown."

Happy didn't last long out my window, so I didn't get an accurate count of the trees there.

But there weren't many. Small boys probably have to take a number and wait in order to climb one.

Until my trip from Lubbock to Amarillo I had taken trees pretty much for granted.

Atlanta has thousands of trees. Millions. There's probably a couple of trees for everybody in town.

A visitor came to Atlanta once and called it "a city in a park."

I'm partial to the dogwoods in Atlanta. Abloom, they are awesome. I will take even more notice henceforth.

I had played golf at the Lubbock Country Club earlier in the day. The course was covered in trees.

"Why are there so many trees here and so few everywhere else?" I asked.

"There's not a tree on the golf course," a member answered, "that a human didn't plant."

Ronald Reagan blamed trees for polluting the air. Fires are claiming acres and acres of them in the West. We chop them down and, among other things, make newsprint out of them.

But you see a place that stands so in need of trees and you realize every time one falls the Earth has lost a precious jewel.

I sound like an environmental freak. Next, I'll probably start whining about whales.

So I asked a woman in Amarillo, Ruth Scamerhorn, who works for the local paper, "What's it like to live where there's such a scarcity of trees?"

"The best way I can describe it," she said, "is this way: A prisoner broke out of the county jail and three days later the paper called the sheriff to see if the escapee had been captured. The sheriff said, 'What's the hurry? I can still see him running.'"

September 1990

Pet Peeves

Just when you thought there could never be another "ism" to plague us (people who think we are plagued by "isms" are guilty of "ismism"), I've found another one:

Petism.

I found it in an article I was reading about how our language is changing in our never-ending battle to remove various biases and "isms" from the way we speak and write.

You can't say fireman or firewoman or even fireperson anymore. It's simply firefighter, according to the article.

The same goes for mailman, mailwoman or mailperson. To be politically correct one must use mail carrier.

As far as one is concerned, it's the way you stay out of trouble when you want to avoid pronounism, which is using he or she at the wrong time.

But back to petism. If you have a dog or a cat or a horse or an orangutan, a boa constrictor or a duckbilled platypus, you don't refer to any of them as your, for example, pet duckbill platypus.

Pets aren't pets anymore, said the article. They are now animal companions. The word pet, I gather, is awash in sexism. There is the *Penthouse* Pet of the Month, of course, where a popular magazine photographs a woman in the nude to appear in the magazine for a lot of money.

This is blatant sexism, of course, because the woman is handcuffed and forced into the photo session and then she is also forced to take the money. You can't see the handcuffs in the photographs because they have been airbrushed out. Lots of people don't know about that.

At any rate, now all of us, including myself, must deal with petism. I can no longer refer to my dog Catfish, the black Lab, as my pet dog Catfish, the black Lab.

Catfish is now my animal companion. When I refer to my animal companion, the way somebody finds out what kind of animal it is, they must ask me.

"Just exactly what sort of animal companion do you have?" they must ask.

And I answer, "My faithful animal companion is a big black dog."

After reading the article I went to a local pet store to get my animal companion some flea powder. I sought out the owner but I can't tell you if the owner was a man or a woman because that would be sexist.

"Do you know, my good [blank], in order to be politically correct you must now call your establishment an animal companion store?" I asked the animal companion-store owner.

"I didn't know that," said the animal companion-store owner, scratching the animal companion store-owner's head.

"Well, now you do," I continued.

The animal companion-store owner assured me the animal companion-store owner would make the change as soon as the animal companion-store owner could.

So now the section at the grocery store will not be known as the pet-food shelf. It will be the animal companion-food shelf, and the former pet-food industry will be the animal companion-food industry.

What the article didn't say was what should be done about the verb *pet*.

Can I still say, "This morning the first thing I did was pet my animal companion"? Or is pet out altogether? Should I say, "This morning the first thing I did was rub/scratch /caress my animal companion"?

By the way, the animal companion-store owner's name was Ralph.

February 1993

Just Walk On By That Gas Station

We could walk a lot more in this country. That's what I said. We could actually walk more.

If we walk more and drive our cars less, then maybe we could become less dependent on foreign oil so when some sheik of the burning sands decided to take over Lower Oil-richabia, we could ignore him.

There wouldn't be any need to send over our troops and planes, no reason to worry about chemical warfare, no reason to bug Henry Kissinger for interviews, no reason to bring up that nasty word *Armageddon*, no reason to have to pay $87.50 a gallon at the neighborhood Texaco, and no reason for Dan Quayle to say, "Please, George, don't die on me now."

I used to walk all the time. Before I got a bicycle, I had to walk practically everywhere I couldn't convince an adult to drive me.

If I got thirsty and my mother said, "Walk, it'll be good for you," when I asked her to drive me to the store for a big orange, I'd have to hoof it a half-mile there and back.

I even walked all the way to Bobby Entrekin's house one day. It was two miles both ways. He had invited me over to play cowboys and punk rockers.

But it was a pleasant, enlightening experience.

On the way, I saw a dead opossum in the road, I found a pointed rock that could have been an arrowhead, I kicked an empty pork and beans can at least a mile, and I had a lot of time to think about what I wanted to do when I grew up.

I decided the next time an adult asked me about it, I would say, "I want to star in porno films" and see the look that would bring.

But after I got my bike and then got old enough to drive, I gave up walking, as have many of us.

Two of the three times I got married, I drove down the aisle. The other time, I took a cab.

I probably would drive between rooms in my house, but my car won't fit through the front door.

We are slaves to our automobiles and the juice that makes them run and that gets us into harm's way and allows oil companies to make us all feel like a bunch of dipsticks for what we have to pay for gasoline.

Let's all start walking more and driving less. We could start with me.

The convenience store where I buy pork and beans and copies of the *Enquirer* is less than a half-mile away. I could walk there.

I could walk to the Waffle House for my weekly cholesterol I.V.

I could walk to the video store to rent *Naughty Female Attorneys* and *Debbie Does Fargo, North Dakota*, neither of which I had a part in, incidentally.

I could walk to a friend's house to play cowboys and rap groups, and I could walk to my ex-girlfriend's house when I forget I am an insensitive, arrogant, selfish jerk and need to be reminded.

Join me, America. Let's go for a walk and give Ahab the Arab and John D. Rockerperson a bad case of gas.

September 1990

Real Mashed Potatoes Don't Come In Boxes

For weeks, I had been seeing a television commercial for this certain chain of restaurants. The commercial claimed the restaurant served home cooking, "The kind mom used to do."

I'm not going to name the restaurant chain. I've already got one libel suit pending.

But I will say I've spent the nearly three decades since I left the cooking Mama used to do looking for something, anything, that came close to it.

I grew up at a fried chicken, pork chops, pot roast and fresh vegetable table, with corn bread or Mama's homemade biscuits on the side. I must have this sort of food at least once a week or be struck by the dreaded bland-food poisoning.

That's because I have to eat a lot of airline food, as well as hotel food. The airlines and hotels get together each year and plan their menus. Steak au Gristle and Chicken a la Belch.

So I gave this chain a try. I walked into one of its restaurants and looked over the menu. There was no fried chicken or pork chops. But there was country fried steak and pot roast. I decided to go for the pot roast.

"Can I get mashed potatoes and gravy with the pot roast?" I asked the waitress.

"Sure," she answered.

The pot roast was so-so. The gravy was suspect. One bite of the mashed potatoes, and I knew. I called the waitress back over.

"I would take it as a personal favor if you would be perfectly honest with me," I said. "These mashed potatoes came out of a box, didn't they?" The waitress dropped her eyes for a brief second. Then she looked up and said apologetically, "Yes, they did."

I hate mashed potatoes that come out of a box. When God created the mashed potato, I am certain the Bible points out somewhere, he had no intention of anybody goofing around and coming up with mashed potatoes from a box.

He meant for real potatoes to be used. You peel them, you cut them into little pieces and put them in a pot of boiling water. You put in some salt and pepper, and then you add some butter and maybe even a little sour cream and then you beat them and stir them and you've got biblically correct mashed potatoes.

I realized the waitress didn't have anything to do with the fact that the restaurant served mashed potatoes from a box in a place that advertised mama's cooking, an affront to mothers everywhere. That was upper management's doing.

So when I paid my bill — reluctantly, due to the fact there should have been a warning on the menu that the mashed potatoes weren't really mashed potatoes — I did have a word with the assistant manager, who took my money anyway.

"May the Lord forgive you for ye know not what you do, you potato ruiner."

I think he thought I was some sort of religious nut. He was still waiting for me to hand him a pamphlet and ask him for money as I walked out the door.

Mashed potatoes from a box. That's what's wrong with this country.

That and non-alcoholic beer, instant grits, canned biscuits, soybean anything, frozen French fries, fake flowers, staged photo opportunities for politicians running for re-election, tanning salons, and I bought some Haagen Dazs vanilla ice cream at the grocery store recently, but when I went to eat it, I realized I had gotten yogurt instead.

What's real anymore? Computerized voices talk to me at the airport.

I phone a friend and I talk to a machine. Musical stars are lip-synching.

Did somebody mention silicone implants? As soon as I make the world safe from boxed mashed potatoes, I'll get around to that.

It's a matter of priorities, you know.

February 1992

A Man, His Dog And His Truck

A few years ago I went out and bought myself one of those sexy convertible imports. Maybe it was a crisis of middle life.

Maybe I thought owning such an automobile would take away notice of the creeping years. A guy driving a sexy convertible import — a flashy red one — is conquering hills in a metallic blur, not going over them into the land of arthritis and prunes on the other side.

The trouble was the car never quite fit me. Perfume on a hog, that sort of thing.

I looked and felt out of place in it. People would see me in it and look at me as if to say, "Look at that old man driving his kid's car."

Or they would say, "Look at that person having a middle-age crisis.

"Why doesn't he get a Lincoln and join the AARP?" I was terribly fastidious about the car as well. I wouldn't even allow my dog Catfish, the black Lab, to ride in it.

I was afraid he would drool on the expensive leather seats or leave a hair. He would look at me as if to say, "You love that stupid car more than you do me."

One morning I went out and found a flat tire on my sexy convertible import. It looked like something had gnawed the air out of it.

The good news here is I no longer have that car. I traded it. I did what very few people have ever done. I traded my flashy red, sexy convertible import for a truck.

I think it was a sign I am over any crisis of middle age and that I am aging gracefully and that I am a mature individual.

I had a truck once before. The speedometer went out when it had 120,000 on it. I drove it another two years before it finally rolled over on its back one day and passed away.

I didn't worry about Catfish drooling or getting hair in that truck. That's what trucks are for.

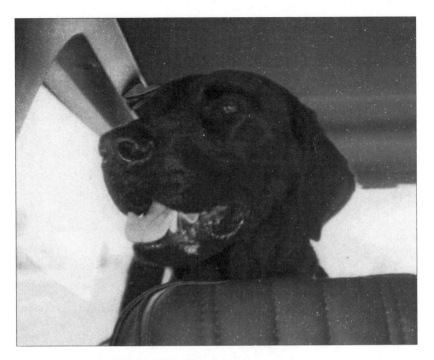

Lewis's beloved Catfish riding proudly in their truck.

But instead of getting another truck, I went for the import, and it has taken me this long to come to my senses.

The guy made me a pretty good deal. I did find out that fourteen minutes after you purchase a sexy convertible import, it loses about sixty percent of its value.

"This is all this car is worth now?" I asked when told what it would bring. "My dog never set foot in it."

The guy showed me the book that lists what cars are worth.

"Best I can do," he said, jingling the change in his pocket. When a car dealer starts jingling the change in his pocket, he knows he's got you.

But it's a pretty truck. I got red again. It's got everything on it but a CD player, which I didn't want anyway because I don't own any CDs, and even if I did, the CD player probably would break or my CDs would become the first in history to rot.

But I've got a tape deck, a radio, air conditioning, power windows and locks and there's a luggage rack on top. Catfish gnaws one tire on my new truck and he rides up there.

I went on my first drive. For the first time in years, I felt comfortable on the road again. I felt like an adult, not some twenty-four-year-old with the top down, the wind blowing through his flowing locks as he cruises for girls who pop their gum and use "goes" in place of "says."

My new truck is American-made, too. I feel a lot better about that.

And it will save on gas, which will help me pay my fair share of taxes after getting so filthy rich during the Reagan and Bush years.

I took Catfish on my first ride in the new truck. He sat right up there in the front seat and drooled and shed happily away.

But we were a team again. A man, a dog, and a truck. All is right with my world.

Nobody can tax that. Can they?

August 1993

CHAPTER

Fourteen

"March 20, 1994: The night the lights went out in Georgia."

WILLIAM E. MAGUIRE
ROSWELL, GEORGIA

A Date That Can't Wait

I sat in the room across from the two doctors at Emory University Hospital. One was wearing his green surgical outfit. The other, a doctor's white coat.

Earlier, the doctor in the white coat had taken pictures of my heart with a machine called an echocardiogram. The machine is able to display the heart on a screen by using sound waves. The procedure doesn't hurt, one of the few such procedures in medicine.

The three of us were meeting to pick a date, a date for my third heart surgery in eleven years.

I had my first in 1982 to replace the faulty aortic valve I appeared with in October of 1946 in Fort Benning, Georgia.

They replaced my old valve with a tissue valve that came from a pig. I was home in six days.

I went to the Soviet Union in 1985. While there, one of my wisdom teeth became infected. The infection went to my valve.

The way they tell it now, I beat death back home by about three days.

This same surgeon operated again and put in another pig valve.

I've known for over two years this day would come. The present pig valve, because it had to be installed in such an infectious environment, is leaking and causing me to be severely anemic.

About two years ago, I went to bed one night weighing 180. The next morning I weighed 160.

People were always asking me, "Did you drive here?" I suddenly looked that frail.

I couldn't list all the unpleasant things I had rather go through than my third heart surgery. Amputation of both my big toes is right up there, however. So is having to move back to Chicago.

The first time I had the surgery I didn't know what to expect. The second time, I was too sick to care.

But this time I will be aware of it all. I know where all those tubes will go. I know how much it will hurt to have the two in my stomach pulled out.

I know all about the lady who comes by your room after surgery and tries to convince you to cough in order to clear your lungs. You can't imagine how much you don't want to cough after somebody has just opened up your chest.

And I know about that damned shave. A man comes into your room the night before your surgery and shaves you from your neck to your knees.

It's embarrassing and it's degrading.

And I know of the anticipation of the week before the surgery. It is all-encompassing.

No more pig valves for me this time, they say. Pig valves, safe from problems with blood-clotting, don't last very long. This time, I will receive the St. Jude's mechanical valve. I will have to take blood thinners to reduce the possibility of blood clots.

But if all goes well, the valve, said my surgeon, should last me the rest of my life.

I was lifted by the surgeon's confidence.

"You'll do fine," he said. My greatest concern, of course, is a third heart operation might kill me.

"You're not going to die," the surgeon said, and then he told me about a lady he would operate on later in the day who was in her seventies and had a lot more problems than me. The surgeon said he expected all to go well with her, too.

I have to look at it this way: At least there is something they can do. Patients with inoperable problems would love to have the chance I do of total recovery.

The doctors told me I could be back on the golf course in eight weeks. I'm shooting for six. The surgeon said, "You'll be surprised how much better you'll feel."

We compared our calendars. March 22.

February 1993

A Miracle Drug
Called Prayer

All those learned men and women of medicine with the eye charts on the end of their names said basically the same thing to me once I had emerged from wherever God puts your mind while people are trying to save your life in a hospital.

They said it was a miracle I had lived from what were the most complicated of complications that arose during what was supposed to have been a fairly routine heart valve replacement surgery at Emory University Hospital six weeks ago.

All I know is what I read in the papers later and what friends and these medical people told me. But it does seem I spent days sticking one foot in and out of death's door.

To a man and woman, those doctors and nurses said to me after the critical time had passed, "We exhausted all medical possibilities. We did everything we knew to do for you, and it probably wouldn't have been enough. What saved you was prayer."

Can you believe that? Great men and women of science saying such a thing in 1993? Prayer? Surely not. It had to be some new miracle drug developed by researchers at Harvard. It had to be one of those cardiac pumps they said they attached to my heart when it just up and decided not to beat any more.

No, they said, it was prayer.

One doctor explained, "Everywhere I went during your worst time, I ran into people who said they were praying for you. One woman said, 'I don't agree with anything he writes, but I'm still praying for him.' A friend said his church held a special prayer service for you. You had a lot of people asking that you be spared."

What I did to deserve any of that, I don't know; but I do know I'd spent a lot of time in my life doubting. At one time or the other, I doubted it all — spirituality, love, the basic goodness of humankind.

But this flirtation with the end of me has removed a lot of

that doubt. If the medical experts say prayer brought me back from certain death, who am I to doubt them? And prayer only works if there is someone or something to grant the favor asked. My faith and belief in that someone or something not only has been restored but it has been forevermore cast in my soul as the great truth beyond all others.

But now comes the hard part. I owe a lot of thank-yous. I must thank those who are responsible for the fact I'm still amongst the quick. The Emory doctors and nurses know how I feel about them. They are the best of the best.

But what do I do about the prayerful? Say simply, "Hey, everybody who prayed for me, thanks"? It's got to be more profound than that. I snatched away a new life.

I have been to the other side of the veil and came back from behind it. I received the reprieve at the midnight hour. I made the dawn once more and it was bright and beckoned with the promise I could finish the unfinished and fulfill the unfulfilled.

Here is what I would like to do: I would like to gather in the parking lot of Atlanta Stadium all who lifted a voice when I stood in need of it so badly and, one by one, I would like to hug them around the neck and say, "I love you and I thank you for my life."

It would be difficult with my history of gentle criticism of Atlanta's city government to get a permit for such a thing, and palm-greasing isn't my style.

So, I suppose I am left with only one recourse. And that is to pray, myself, and ask, "Lord, you know who you heard from in my behalf. Please let them know there is no end to my gratitude."

And, for the record, even if you didn't pray for me, it's nice to be with you again, too.

To be honest, it's just nice to be.

May 1993

No Mind To Go

Inquiring minds want to know, "Lewis, what's it like to come close to dying?" I did, in fact, do that — come close to dying. My own doctor said, "You were as good as gone."

The man has a way with words.

Several weeks ago the idea was to put a new aortic valve in my heart at Emory University Hospital, which surgeons accomplished. The problem arose when my heart wouldn't start beating on its own again after it had been stilled for the operation and its role had been taken over by a machine.

It was a touchy few days.

"They told us," said a friend, " 'It doesn't look good,' but their eyes and faces said it was over."

But here I am. Miracles happen.

What's it like to come close to dying? I really don't know. While all that was going on, while friends and family said they were going through the anguish of it all, I wasn't around.

My bloated old body was, but my mind — set free of the pain and the dread by whatever it was they were shooting in my veins — wasn't even in the same vicinity or time period.

They could have given me a head transplant and I'd never have known it.

I was even in World War II at one point while they carved away on me.

Get this dream vision: Eisenhower himself called me to his command post during the war in 1943 and told me some of Hitler's generals wanted to surrender, but they couldn't convince the Fuhrer.

Ike, knowing how many Discovery and Arts & Entertainment Channel World War II black and white documentaries I had watched, put me in charge of finding a way to convince Hitler it was useless to continue the war against the Allies.

Piece of cake. I found a few of the scientists who would

later work on the Manhattan Project and develop the atomic bomb and got them to draw me a picture of what one looked like. I showed it to Hitler's generals, and they took it back to the Fuhrer, who called off the war and there wasn't even a Normandy invasion.

And another La-La Land experience: British golf officials came to me and explained they might have to call off the British Open because it was a tradition each year's champion must drink a special grog, the recipe for which had been lost, and you know how the British are about tradition.

That was easy, too. I located an old woman living in a back alley in St. Andrews, Scotland, who had the recipe and I saved the Open. A damned fine grog it was, too, incidentally.

I had no out-of-body experiences. I saw no bright lights that I followed into a tunnel. I heard no angels singing.

On the other hand, I got no whiff of smoke, either, something to be avoided at all costs when one is hovering near the ultimate embarkation point.

There was never any fear. Never any dread. There were no warning bells, nor voices of instruction regarding a journey's end and perhaps another's beginning.

I didn't see God, I didn't see the Devil, and please don't be tacky enough to ask about Elvis.

I guess all that is a good thing. Had I closed on that proverbial piece of rural property (croaked), it would have been a peaceful, no-hassle exit — for me, at least. And what did the gambler say: "The best you can hope for is to die in your sleep"? So, if I had died, that would have been a piece of cake, too.

But when have I ever taken the easy way out of anything? Coming close to dying was a snap. Living the rest of my life surrounded by everybody and his brother-in-law who is suddenly a health expert is going to be the hard part.

May 1993

Of Rockin' Chairs, Power Walkers And Catfish

I've been doing a lot of sitting on my front porch lately. I do this late in the evenings after the intense summer heat has subsided.

I suppose there are two primary reasons. One is, television just gets more rotten by the day. I've got fifty channels, and I still have trouble finding anything worth watching. I'm even tired of the Spice Channel. The plots simply never change.

I also come from a long line of front-porch sitters, and before air-conditioning and television, that's the way a lot of people used to spend their evenings.

I did that with my own family when I was growing up. My grandfather and I used to count cars and listen for trains.

I've been sitting on my front porch with my dog Catfish, the black Lab. I count BMWs. He growls when Volvos come by.

I live on a nice street and I have a nice front porch. I have a swing and two rocking chairs. I sit in one of the rocking chairs.

The swing is a little hard on what is left of my rear following the weight loss I incurred as a result of my heart surgery in March.

One thing I have noticed is there are a lot of other people, at least in my neighborhood, who aren't sitting inside watching television in the evenings, either. They aren't sitting on their porches, however.

They are out engaging in some sort of exercise.

There aren't just joggers anymore. In fact, there seems to be fewer joggers everyday.

(I was sitting in my doctor's office a few weeks ago when a nurse looked in and said to him, "CNN is on the phone. They want to know your advice on running in the Peachtree Road Race in this hot weather." My doctor looked up and said, "Don't. A man had a heart attack and died in that race.")

A lot of bicycle riders come by my house while Catfish and I are on the porch. They wear helmets and tight pants and race past in large packs. The other evening, maybe fifteen came by in a blur. Three minutes later a lone cyclist raced past. He appeared to be attempting to catch up with the others.

"He reminds me of horses I tend to bet on," I said to Catfish.

I get a lot of people out walking their dogs. A man comes by walking a dog that looks like a rat. He sort of looks like a rat, too. They say people often begin resembling their pets after a time.

Catfish and I have been together for over a decade, but my ears seem to be the same length as always.

I get roller skaters. They tend to be younger than the other exercisers. A roller skater came by my house recently, going downhill, at what must have been thirty-five miles an hour. If he had fallen, they would have had to scrape him up.

There's another group that comes by my house that is exercising in a manner to which I am not familiar.

They aren't jogging, but they aren't simply strolling, either. They are walking very fast and slinging their arms back and forth.

"That's power walking," somebody told me. "It's not as hard on your knees as jogging."

It looks like prissing to me, but I'm nearly fifty and don't own a Nordic Trac.

It once was the custom to speak pleasantly to anybody who happened to come past while one was sitting on one's porch. I wondered how that would play in a large American city in the '90s.

So one night whenever the joggers, power walkers or dog walkers would come by (the roller skaters and cyclists were going too fast,) I would call out, "Good evening."

Amazing. To a person, each called back, "Good evening."

I must have said "Good Evening" twenty times, and not once did anybody ignore my attempt to be pleasant.

That made me feel awfully good. Made me feel good about myself, my neighbors and my city.

We may even take up front-porch sitting full time, me and ol' Catfish. He said he thought the power walkers looked like they were prissing, too, by the way.

We don't look alike, but I guess we're starting to think alike as we enter our rocking-chair years.

July 1993

Shut-In
But Not Shut Down

Remember back in church when they used to ask you to pray for the shut-ins? I was never quite certain what a shut-in was.

I went ahead and prayed for them anyway, but what was a shut-in? Somebody they had to keep boarded up like a dog that was bad to chase cars? So for all of this time I didn't even know what a shut-in was, and, then, I became one.

For the past two and a half months I have, in fact, been a shut-in.

It took me four months to get over last spring's harrowing heart surgery. My chest healed. My legs stopped hurting and my feet stopped swelling.

I even went back to the golf course. My partners allowed me to play from the ladies' tees at the beginning. I had to endure a lot of remarks regarding various female problems I might be having as a result of my move to what I learned to refer to as the "forward tees," but, quite comfortable in my masculinity, I ignored them as mere chirpings of sexist pork.

Then my side started hurting. I thought it might be a yeast infection.

Turned out it was this: During my heart surgery I had been wired for a pacemaker in case I happened to need one during my recovery period.

Surgeons created a small pouch to the left of my navel for the wires. The wires became infected. The pouch became infected.

I became a shut-in.

I couldn't play golf. I couldn't walk. I couldn't sit up. For two months my doctors attempted to treat the problem with antibiotics.

But the infection wouldn't go away. So, a week ago, I went back to Emory University Hospital and surgeons removed the wires. The infection is gone.

In a couple of more weeks I'm supposed to be completely healed and a seven-month ordeal finally will be over. But what an ordeal. If I had known what the life of a shut-in was all about, I would have prayed a lot harder for them.

You just sit there a lot. You sleep. You work crossword puzzles. You watch "The Streets of San Francisco" afternoon reruns on cable. You talk on the telephone.

"How you feelin'?"

"'Bout the same."

"Anything I can do?"

"Yeah, tell Karl Malden to get a nose job."

What saved me was the Atlanta Braves. I watched every inning of every game they played the last two months of the season.

Otis Nixon made that catch over the centerfield wall night after night on the WTBS promos. Sid Bream always scored that run against Pittsburgh and the Braves won, the Braves won, the Braves won, the Braves won, the Braves won!

I played the AFLAC trivia game. I saw that guy break his leg night after night at the company picnic softball game.

"Got any ideas?"

"Yeah, AFLAC."

I did everything but enter the Goody's Home Run Jackpot. Kent Mercker would have batted for me.

I saw the press-box fire and I agreed with Don Sutton that "McRip" would be a better nickname for Fred McGriff than "Crime Dog." Fred never chased a car in his life.

Rafael Belliard, by the way, saved the West Division pennant when he played like an all-star when Mark Lemke was out at second base. Lest we forget.

And each time they showed the Giants dugout, I noticed Dusty Baker drinking bottled water. Dry mouth got the Giants.

I suppose what I'm doing here is thanking the Braves for the memories. Without them, what might I have done? Fallen into a deep well of depression? Called radio talk shows? Gone back to the vodka?

Pray for those who remain as shut-ins. Baseball season will soon be over.

October 1993

He Up And Died And Broke My Heart

My dog Catfish, the black Lab, died Thanksgiving night. The vet said his heart gave out.

Down in the country, they would have said, "Lewis's dog up and died."

He would have been twelve had he lived until January.

Catfish had a good life. He slept indoors. Mostly he ate what I ate. We shared our last meal Tuesday evening in our living room in front of the television.

We had a Wendy's double cheeseburger and some chili.

Catfish was a gift from my friends Barbara and Vince Dooley. Vince, of course, is the athletic director at the University of Georgia. Barbara is a noted speaker and author.

I named him driving back to Atlanta from Athens where I had picked him up at the Dooleys's home. I don't know why I named him what I named him. He was all curled up in a blanket on my back seat. And I looked at him and it just came out. I called him, "Catfish."

I swear he raised up from the blanket and acknowledged. Then he severely fouled the blanket and my back seat.

He was a most destructive animal the first three years of his life.

He chewed things. He chewed books. He chewed shoes.

"I said to Catfish, 'Heel,'" I used to offer from behind the dais, "and he went to my closet and chewed up my best pair of Guccis."

Catfish chewed television remote-control devices. Batteries and all.

He chewed my glasses. Five pairs of them.

One day, when he was still a puppy, he got out of the house without my knowledge. The doorbell rang. It was a young man who said, "I hit your dog with my car, but I think he's OK."

He was. He had a small cut on his head and he was frightened, but he was otherwise unhurt.

"I came around the corner," the young man explained, "and he was in the road chewing on something. I hit my brakes the second I saw him."

"Could you tell what he was chewing on?" I asked.

"I know this sounds crazy," the young man answered, "but I think it was a beer bottle."

Catfish stopped chewing while I still had a house. Barely.

He was a celebrity, Catfish. I spoke recently in Michigan. Afterwards a lady came up to me and said, "I was real disappointed with your speech. You didn't mention Catfish."

Catfish used to get his own mail. Just the other day the manufacturer of a new brand of dog food called "Country Gold," with none other than George Jones's picture on the package, sent Catfish a sample of its new product. For the record, he still preferred cheeseburgers and chili.

Catfish was once grand marshal of the Scottsboro, Alabama, "Annual Catfish Festival." He was on television and got to ride in the front seat of a police car with its siren on.

He was a patient, good-natured dog, too. Jordan, who is five, has been pulling his ears since she was two. She even tried to ride him at times. He abided with nary a growl.

Oh, that face and those eyes. What he could do to me with that face and those eyes. He would perch himself next to me on the sofa in the living room and look at me.

And love and loyalty would pour out with that look, and as long as I had that, there was very little the human race could do to harm my self-esteem.

Good dogs don't love bad people.

He was smart. He was fun. And he loved to ride in cars. There were times he was all that I had.

And now he has up and died. My own heart, or what is left of it, is breaking.

November 1993

Memories Of Catfish Keep On Doggin'

It's been two months since my dog, Catfish, the black Lab, up and died on me.

He would have been twelve this month. I really thought I would be over it all by now. I get over divorces and surgeries in about six months. I figured I could get over the death of a dog in two.

But he lingers.

I've been asked a thousand times, "Are you going to get a new dog?" I thought about it, and I've had a lot of offers. For all I hear about the failings of the human race, there are yet so many still out there that are willing to step forward in another's time of need. Even strangers.

I've had offers of bulldogs, beagle hounds, even a poodle, perish the thought, and, of course, other black Labs. I heard from a woman with a new litter of black Labs that had a paper trail on them dating back a century.

I'm sorry. I just didn't want a dog with a more impressive pedigree than my own.

And I worry about bringing up another dog during a puppy stage. I have a friend who was telling me, "My wife and I got a puppy once who chewed up our driveway."

I didn't believe that.

"I'm not lying," said my friend. "The dog chewed up the driveway. He found one loose piece of asphalt and started there. He pulled out that piece and chewed on it and then another piece and then another, until he had chewed-up asphalt chunks all over the yard and our driveway was dirt."

Catfish, when he was a puppy, destroyed television remote-control devices and my eyeglasses.

I miss his companionship. I had my place on the green couch in front of the television. His place was next to me. He would sprawl there and sleep like some kingly beast upon his padded divan as long as I would remain next to him. And that was his place. Anyone who dared take it while he was temporarily away would be met with a wretched stare and a bark when Catfish wanted it back.

And they would move. I doubt he actually would have bitten them if they hadn't, but they didn't know that, and, come to think about it, I'm not absolutely certain he wouldn't have, either.

Evidence of him remains around the house. I found a chewed-up golf ball on the floor the other day. That was his doing.

Catfish grew out of the destructive stage at three, but he would still maim something like an occasional golf ball if he happened to find it on the floor.

His bag of food is still in the cupboard. I've just never gotten around to throwing it out.

There's still a framed photograph of me holding him when he was a puppy in the den hallway. When he was alive I rarely noticed it. Now it seems to catch my eye each time I walk past it.

I miss him at night. I've got one of those elaborate alarm systems, but I'd felt even safer knowing that nothing would approach my house without meeting with Catfish's bark, which was astoundingly deep and loud.

And I miss that bark when I come home. It never mattered what time I came home or where I had been. As soon as he would hear the car door slam in the driveway, he would start and he would keep it up until I opened the door. And then, there he would stand, tail awag, to greet me. My self-esteem always soared.

I walk into an empty, silent house these days. I feel the difference in the deepest recesses of wherever it is my love resides.

Two months. No whining and pawing on the door to go outside. No thrilled bellow at the words, "Catfish, wanna go for a ride?" No smell.

Dogs smell. It was a good smell.

Two months. Sixty days. It should have ended by now.

I said, it should have.

January 1994

A *Happy* New *Year* To *Me*; I *Endured* '93

I am currently being held hostage at Emory University Hospital by an IV pole. As we speak, I am plotting my escape.

There are several bags of medicine hanging at the top of my pole.

From each bag a tube runs into a central tube that leads to a needle that is stuck inside the top of my left wrist. That is how the medicine gets into my blood stream. I'm not certain exactly what each medicine is. One rather large bag resembles a rhinoceros udder. It is filled with a white, milky substance.

Another has what looks like Mrs. Butterworth's syrup inside it, while a third is some sort of antibiotic substance — a sort of Orkin-Man-in-a-bag to ward off any bugs that might want to encamp in my innards.

Whither I goest, goest my IV pole, but we don't goest very far. The six steps from my bed to my bathroom is about the limit of how far Ivy and I can travel. We'd look silly at a Karaoke bar singing "Don't Fence Me In" together anyway.

What's wrong with me is I'm sick. That's what my doctor said.

"You're sick," he said.

"And what's the plan of treatment?" I asked him.

"We're going to attach you to a pole until you get better," he explained.

I'll try to keep this simple: I have to take a prescribed blood thinner, because I have an artificial aortic valve in my heart.

But a few weeks ago my blood became much too thin because I also took a large amount of a blood-thinning over-the-counter painkiller in an attempt to treat lower back pain I encountered during a venture around the country promoting and signing a book I wrote.

My blood became so thin that I bled internally, which is very dangerous and caused the most severe pain I've ever known.

Until my blood is back to where doctors want it to be, until I stop hurting, I'm stuck here with this pole. But I'm trying to make the best of it and look upon what is certainly a recently brightened side of my existence.

Yes, I'm in the hospital. But I didn't have to get the tux cleaned for a New Year's Eve party.

I had the time to read Rush Limbaugh's second book, *See, I Told You So*, another masterpiece, and you don't need to change underwear but every other day in the hospital.

And even more thrilling is the knowledge 1993 is finally over. I am certain that it is. Dick Clark said so on the television in my hospital room.

We have, in fact, Auld Lang Syned that ball of personal anguish into history's waste dump and, for me, it was about time. 1993 was the worst year of the forty-seven I have lived.

In 1993:

I had heart surgery and nearly died.

I had another surgery to remove infected pacemaker wiring.

I had whatever it is I have now.

My dog died.

My taxes were raised.

My alma mater's football team, the Georgia Bulldogs, had a losing season.

My favorite baseball team, the Braves, had the best record in either league after the regular season and didn't even make it to the World Series.

Bill.

Hillary.

But 1993 is over. It's got to get better. Got to.

"Can't get no worse," friends have said.

My resolutions are few, but my determination is boundless.

I am going to get unattached from this pole. I am going to get well and get out of this hospital and stay out. When that is achieved, I am going somewhere it is warm for a long time.

I survived 1993. 1994 has finally arrived.

Happy New Year to me.

January 1994

Home At Last

It isn't easy getting out of a hospital, even after a doctor says you can go.

I had been at Emory for two weeks. There are veteran lab rats that haven't undergone the testing I did. Name an orifice and somebody put a tube in it.

The worst was what they call a TEE. You swallow a garden hose.

I was bleeding into my liver. A doctor ran a catheter up an artery from my groin and stopped the bleeding. Otherwise they told me later the repairs would have had to have been done surgically and what with my blood so thin, well. . . .

The doctor said, "Go home and eat."

The blood loss and hospital stay have taken me down to what I haven't weighed since I started shaving.

They wouldn't just let me walk out of the hospital. I think they were afraid I would fall down or the wind from a door shutting might blow me down.

So, before I could go, they had to call Transportation for a wheelchair to get me to the parking lot where somebody waited to drive me home.

I packed and waited for Transportation on the side of the bed. How many hours had I stared at that print entitled "Impressions of America" on the wall? The tray from lunch was still there. So was the food on it. They bring the meals and when you take the cover off the entree, water from the collected steam inside drips into the entree, spoiling whatever appetite you might have had.

Twenty-four hours times fourteen, I'd been in that room. The last minutes passed like kidney stones.

Even after Transportation had seated me in the rolling chair, I still had to pass the nurses stand.

That was fine. I had wanted to say goodbye. I hadn't always been pleasant or cooperative, but I guess they're used to that.

I said goodbye and thanks.

A nurse gave me a form to sign.

To the elevator and down. And out to the parking lot and, finally, into the car and toward home.

It was the first time I had been anywhere except inside a hospital in 1994.

I missed the dog greeting me at the front door. He's been dead nearly two months now. The papers had piled up on the front porch. There was lots of mail.

"You get home and you'll feel a lot better," people told me.

It's better than the hospital. Nobody takes my vital signs every three hours. Anybody who comes at me for blood in my house will be met by a steak knife from my kitchen drawer.

They didn't have cable at the hospital. I've got over fifty channels at home. I can watch Purdue play basketball against the University of Connecticut — or was it Seton Hall? — in the privacy of my own den now.

Gerrie cooked me pork chops. A man sent chicken and dumplings and turnip greens. I sent out for chili dogs. James brought me Wendy's. My friend Spike came by one morning and made breakfast. Spike can fry eggs to my liking like nobody since my mother. And I try to eat. I really try to eat.

The medicine is still there. Big pills. Little pills. You take one of these a day. Two of these a day. Then there's that green iron pill I take three times a day that's supposed to replace the blood I lost.

I hate taking pills.

My bed is the best part of being home. There is actually room to turn over in it.

I don't want to go back to a hospital. Ever. Since March 22, 1993, I've spent three months in a hospital. That's enough. Isn't that enough? One doctor says two or three weeks to get back. Another says six to eight.

I just want to live my normal life again.

I'm home. I guess that's a start.

January 1994